PRICE ACTION TRADING SECRETS REVEALED

Become a consistently profitable trader, using proven price action techniques

Includes case studies of 50+ charts post 2020

Akshay Kore

SCAN FOR BONUS

notionpress.com

INDIA • SINGAPORE • MALAYSIA

ISBN 979-8-89026-886-0

Acknowledgements :

As I pen down this section, my heart is filled with immense gratitude and warmth for all those who stood by me during the creation of this book **"Price Action Trading Secrets Revealed".**

First and foremost, I owe an eternal debt of gratitude to my family, my pillars of strength, and my reservoirs of encouragement. To my father, Mr. Suresh Kore, whose principles have always directed me; to my mother, Mrs. Hema Kore, whose love and blessings have been the wind beneath my wings; to my elder brother, Mr. Mithun Kore, who has been a constant source of inspiration; to my sister-in-law, Mrs. Sneha Raut-Kore, for her unwavering faith in me; and last but certainly not least, to my beloved wife, Dr. Runali Kelwalkar-Kore, who has been my anchor and confidante, whose insights, patience, and enduring love shaped every page of this book.

A special thanks to TradingView for providing the insightful charts that have enhanced this book's clarity and to Screener.in for their invaluable scanner screenshots, which added an extra layer of depth to the content.

Ms. Mausumi Devi, the owner of Grafitoon, deserves a distinct mention. Your artistry and design acumen have transformed the pages of this book into a visual delight, perfectly complementing the technical depth within. Your touch of elegance has been invaluable.

Finally, a deep note of appreciation for Notion Press. Their trust, expertise, and dedication ensured that my vision transcended from thought to tangible text.

To all, named and unnamed, who contributed to this venture, my heart brims with thanks. Together, we've sculpted a narrative that I hope resonates with every reader.

With sincere gratitude,

Akshay Suresh Kore

Preface:

As a Certified Technical Analyst & an Equity Derivatives Analyst, I have had the privilege of trading in the financial markets including the commodities & currency market for over 8 years. Over the years, I have developed and refined my trading approach and techniques, and I am excited to share my knowledge and experience with you in this book, "Price Action Trading Secrets Revealed."

Price action trading is a powerful approach that has stood the test of time. Unlike other trading methods that rely on lagging indicators and complex algorithms, price action trading relies on the interpretation of raw price data to determine potential trading opportunities. This approach is based on the principle that the market price reflects all available information, and the price action itself provides all the signals a trader needs, to make informed decisions.

In this book, I will reveal my secrets to successful price action trading. I will guide you through the fundamental concepts of price action analysis and show you how to identify key price patterns and market structures. You will learn about the role of psychology in trading and how to manage risk effectively, through examples of recent trades. Additionally, I will share over 50+ recent charts post-2020, showing price action trading strategies & position sizing calculator that I have developed and used for my own trading.

This book is designed for traders of all levels, from beginners to seasoned professionals. Whether you are looking to supplement your existing trading method or start from scratch, this book will provide you with the knowledge and skills you need to trade with confidence and profitability.

So, grab a cup of coffee, settle into a comfortable chair, and prepare to unlock the secrets of price action trading!

About the Author

The author of 'Price Action Trading Secrets Revealed', Mr. Akshay Kore is an Engineer by profession and a Trader by passion. He is an NCFM certified Technical Analyst and NiSM certified Equity Derivatives Analyst. **He has also won the Zerodha 60-Day Challenge 12 times cumulatively, across all three segments - Equity F&O, Currency & Commodities.**

The author has a deep understanding of price action analysis and has successfully applied these principles to generate consistent **profits in the Equity & Derivatives market as well as Currency & Commodities market.** Mr. Akshay has a sizable following on Quora, where he has more than 10,000 personal and space followers, thanks to his ability to clearly and concisely explain complicated topics related to trading and finance. He has provided invaluable guidance to novice traders and investors alike, on the knowledge-sharing website Quora, where he has answered over 700 questions having over 4 Million views.

In 'Price Action Trading Secrets Revealed', the author shares his proven approach to price action trading, which is based on years of experience and research. This comprehensive guide covers everything from the basics of price action analysis to advanced techniques for maximizing profits and provides readers with the tools and strategies they need to succeed in the highly competitive world of trading.

Whether you're a beginner or an experienced trader, 'Price Action Trading Secrets Revealed' is an essential resource for anyone looking to improve their understanding of the stock market and become a more successful trader. So if you're ready to take your trading to the next level, pick up your copy today and join the many traders who have already benefited from the author's expertise and insights.

Certifications

Table of Contents

CHAPTER 1
Introduction to Technical Analysis

What is Technical Analysis (TA)?

Technical Analysis (TA) is the art and science of estimating future prices based on the analysis of price movements in the past.

Why you MUST learn Technical Analysis?

You must be thinking, why should you learn so much about Technical Analysis?

Well, the answer is simple!

Technical Analysis is a very effective tool for analyzing price behavior.

How effective is it?

Charles Dow, the co-founder of The Wall Street Journal, one of the world's most respected financial publications, has given three theories for this:

1. Price discounts everything.
2. Price movements are not totally random.
3. What is more important than why.

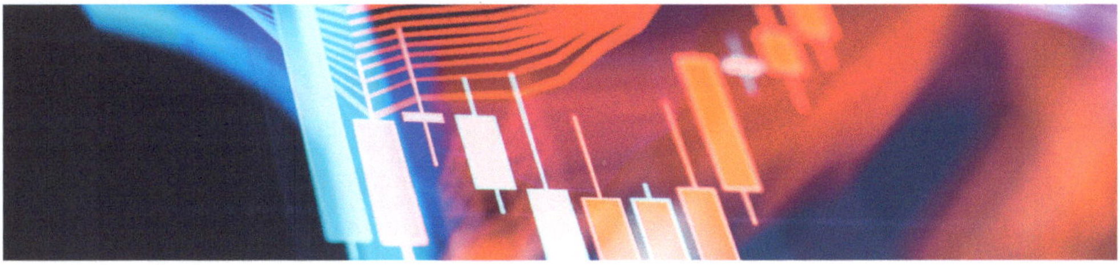

1. Price discounts everything:

It is said that the *"Market knows Everything."*

This is because Technical Analysts believe that the current price of any stock/index fully considers all the possible material information that could affect the price. The market price reflects the collective knowledge of all participants, including traders, investors, portfolio managers, buy-side analysts, sell-side analysts, market strategists, technical analysts, fundamental analysts, and many others. Technical Analysis looks at the price and presumes that it will perform the same way as it did under similar circumstances in the past.

2. Price movements are NOT totally random:

If prices were always random, making money using Technical Analysis would be challenging, right? Fortunately, It's not that way!

Technical Analysis is a trend-following system. Most Analysts agree that hundreds of years of price charts have revealed one fundamental truth – *Prices move in trends.* Therefore, it is possible to identify a trend, trade based on it, and make money as it unfolds. Furthermore, because technical analysis can be applied to diverse time frames, spotting short and long-term trends is possible. It also enables one to find the market's direction.

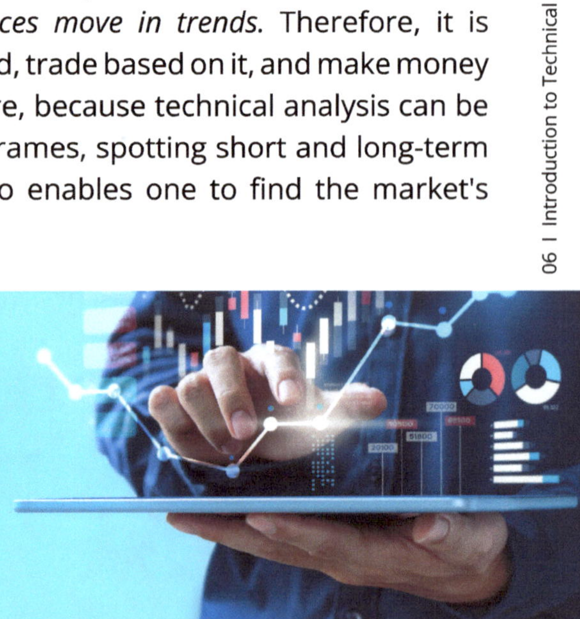

There are only three directions in which the market can move- upward, downward or sideward. Each of these directions is known as a 'trend.' Look at the images below for better clarity (Fig.1.0)

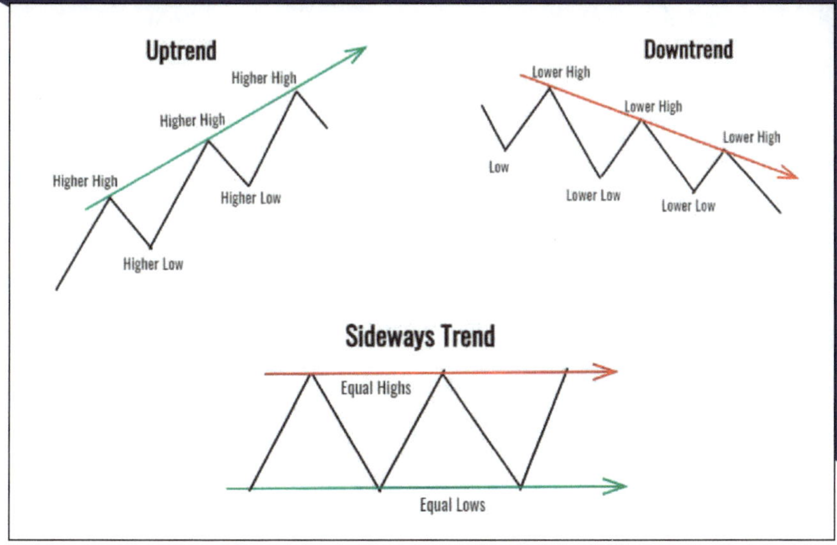

(Fig. 1.0)

3. WHAT is more important than WHY:

Fundamental analysts are concerned only with the WHY, i.e., why the price is what it is. This is right, but a Technical Analyst has a different approach. For a Technical analyst, the answer to WHY is that either buyers are more aggressive than sellers (as seen in a bullish market) or sellers are more aggressive than buyers (as seen in a bearish market). The price is simply the final result of the fight between bulls and bears (buyers and sellers).

Assumptions in Technical Analysis :

There are three main assumptions in Technical Analysis:

1. *Price discounts Everything.*
2. *Price movements are NOT totally random. They are trend based.*
3. *History tends to repeat itself.*

We have seen the first two assumptions in detail already, as it's the same as the first two theories given by Charles Dow.

Now let us understand the third assumption of Technical analysis.

It says that: History tends to repeat itself.

Price movements are repetitive. It is repetitive because, over time, market participants/traders (buyers or sellers) tend to react consistently to similar market stimuli. In the long run, this consistent reaction or psychology of traders is reflected in the price action in the form of patterns. People have been using patterns and charts to show and understand these recurring price action patterns for decades. In technical analysis, chart patterns are utilized to study market movements and understand the trends.

How is Technical Analysis done?

Technical Analysis means plotting stock data, like price, volumes, etc., on a chart and then applying various patterns and indicators to it to determine future price movements.

The period to which one can apply Technical Analysis may vary. For example, it can be used on shorter time frames like 1, 5,10,15,30, or 60 minutes. It can also be used on longer time frames like daily, weekly, monthly, or many years together.

Technical Analysis works on the Pareto principle, which states,

'For many outcomes, roughly 80% of consequences come from 20% of causes'. It is also known as the 80/20 rule.

So a Technical Analyst believes that the market has an 80% psychological component and is only 20% logical or practical. On the other hand, a Fundamental Analyst thinks the exact opposite to be true: the market is only 20% psychological and 80% rational.

Psychological or rational, that's debatable, but the current price of a security is unquestionable! After all, it is there for everyone to see, and nobody doubts its authenticity.

Furthermore, the price set by the market reflects the collective expertise of all the candidates involved, and we are not dealing with featherweights here. These candidates have considered (discounted) everything one can reasonably imagine and then arrived at a price to buy or sell. These are the forces of Buyers and Sellers at play!

Technical Analysis studies price action to understand which force (Buyers or Sellers) is prevailing and focuses directly on the crux of the matter, that is:

What is the price?

Where has it been?

Where is it going?

Takeaways:

- Technical analysis is a way of understanding market movements using price action.
- It involves plotting stock data, like price, volumes, etc., on a chart and then applying various patterns and indicators to it to determine future price movements.
- Price movements are trend-based: uptrend, downtrend, or sideways trend.

CHAPTER 2
Introduction to Price Action Trading & Candlesticks

Price action trading has the same roots as Technical Analysis from the DOW theory, as discussed in chapter 1.

To read price action, you must first understand what it is and what it represents.

Price action is simply the movement of price over time. It is depicted on a chart as a line, candlestick, or bar. Each time period represented on the chart will have its own price action. To read price action, you must first identify the trend.

A trend is the overall direction of the market. It can be up, down, or sideways. Once you have identified the trend, you can look for specific price action signals that will tell you when to enter or exit a trade. There are many different price action signals, but some of the most common ones are:

- Support and resistance levels
- Trend lines
- Candlestick patterns
- Price action divergences.

You can use each of the above signals to make trading decisions. However, it is essential to remember that no signal is 100% accurate. Therefore, they should be used as part of a larger trading system.

When looking at price action, it is also essential to consider *Volume*.

In the stock market, Volume refers to the total quantity of stocks bought and sold by Buyers & Sellers, respectively, in a given period of time (usually one day). It is used to confirm price action signals.

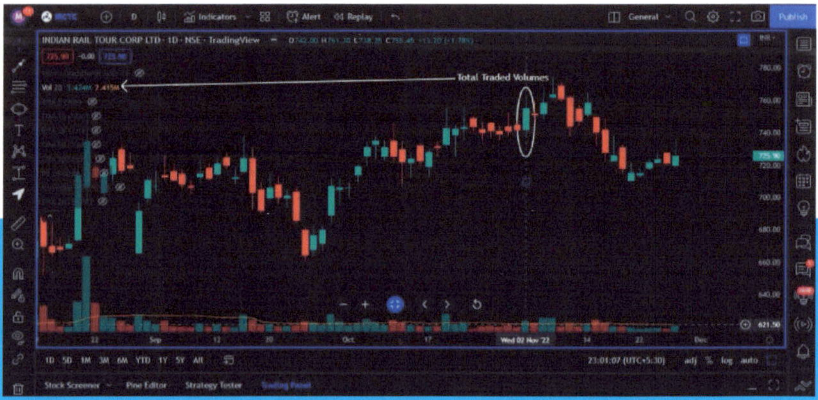

(Fig. 2.1)

The chart above (Fig. 2.1) shows you the total traded volumes on the left hand side of IRCTC chart on 02/11/2022.

3.42 Million Buyers

2.41 Million Sellers

Since the number of Buyers is more than that of Sellers, the volume bar at the bottom is green. Also, the candle is green-coloured since the closing price is more than the opening price.

Market participants, whether Buyers or Sellers, can be broadly classified into two groups :

1. *Reactive Participants*
2. *Active Participants*

Reactive Participants :

These participants are the ones who buy or sell a particular stock when they believe that the stock's current price is far above or far below its fair value. Simply put, they buy a stock when they think it is trading at a much lower value than its fair value. However, their belief is not backed by or supported by any quantitative data. Since they buy stocks based on their preconceived valuation levels, they enter in fewer volumes. As a result, they won't initiate strong buying or selling activity that will lift the price & push them higher. This, in turn, leads to range bound movement & may not break the boundaries set by the stock prices. So by now, reading all this, you must have clearly understood that Reactive players end up on the losing side, almost always.

Active Participants :

It requires powerful & knowledgeable players to move the markets & take the prices higher.

Active participants are the ones who strongly believe that the price of a stock must be above or below the equilibrium created by the Reactive players. Quantitative data back their belief. When such participants enter the market with solid convictions about prices, they are willing to buy even above the upper boundary set by stock prices. Active players buy stocks at higher levels since they firmly believe that new highs will be made by the stock soon. Through their actions, aggression & conviction, they are responsible for the stock prices breaking the given range.

The following image (Fig. 2.2) shows both players.

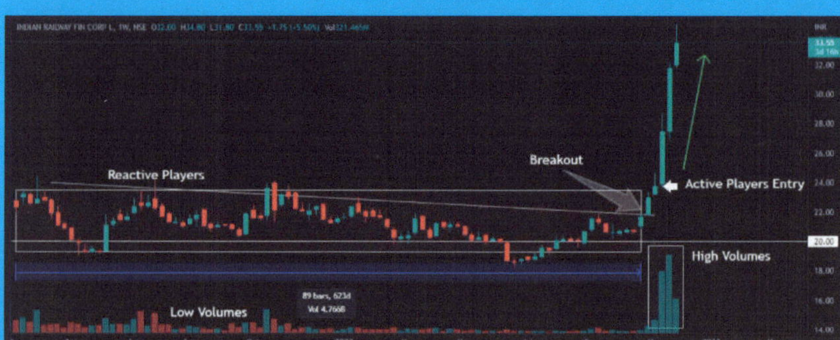

(Fig. 2.2)

Some examples of Active participants may be hedge funds, HNI's, FII's, professionally managed investment funds etc.

Now let us understand Candlesticks in detail.

Candlesticks :

Candlesticks are a visual representation of market price fluctuations & were developed in the 18th Century by Munehisa Homma, a Japanese rice trader.

In a candlestick chart, candles are of two types:

Bullish candle-represented by the colour green.

Bearish candle- represented by the colour red.

Let us have a look at the Bullish candle/candlestick.

A Bullish candlestick is of three components:

The Central Real body: The rectangular body that connects open and close prices.

Upper Shadow: that connects the high point to the close.

Lower Shadow: that connects the low point to the open.

The image (Fig.2.3) will give you clarity about how a bullish candle forms:

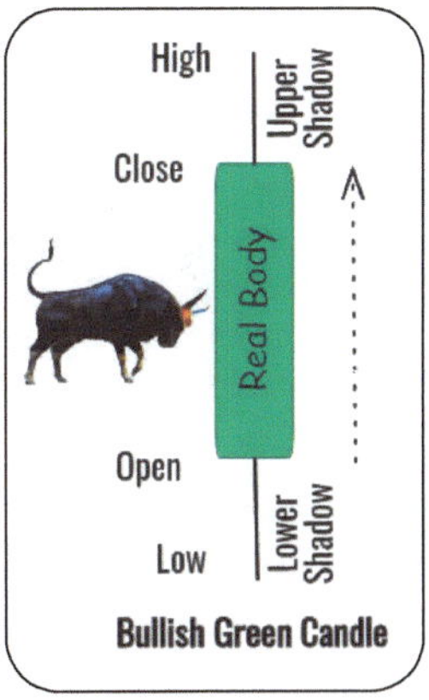

(Fig. 2.3)

The Bearish candle, like the bullish candle, also has three components :

The Central real body: The real rectangular body connects the opening and closing price. Here, the candlestick opens at the top and closes at the rectangle's bottom.

Upper Shadow: Connects the Open to the High point.
Lower Shadow: Connects the Close to the Low point.

This is what a bearish candle would look like (Fig.2.4):

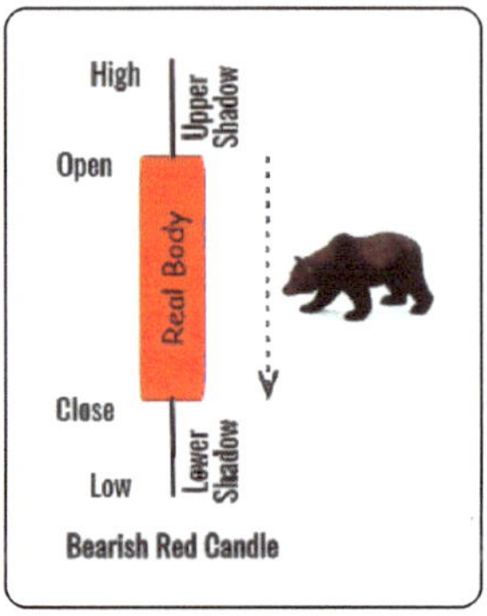

(Fig. 2.4)

Let's understand candlesticks further with the help of stock data for a day.

Eg. On 1st August 2022, Reliance Industries Ltd. Stock had the following prices :

- Open: 2522/-
- High: 2589/-
- Low: 2513/-
- Close: 2575/-

So, how do we get this information from the candlestick? Check out the image (Fig.2.5):

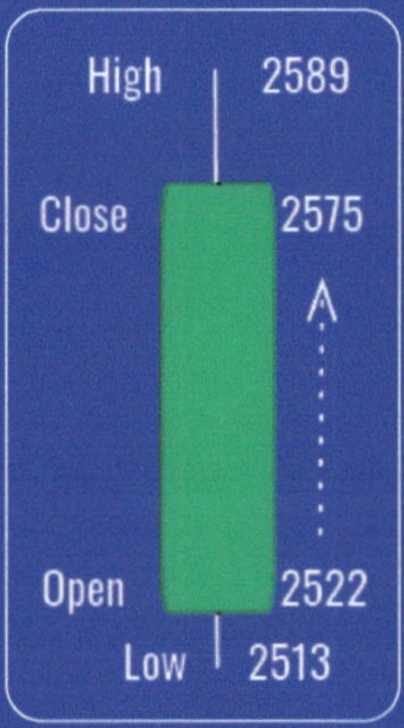

(Fig. 2.5)

Now let's understand the bearish candlestick with the help of a similar example :

E.g., On 1st July 2022, Reliance Industries Ltd. Stock had the following prices :

Open: 2572/-
High: 2589/-
Low: 2360/-
Close: 2412/-

So, how is this information plotted on the candlestick? Check out the image (Fig.2.6) :

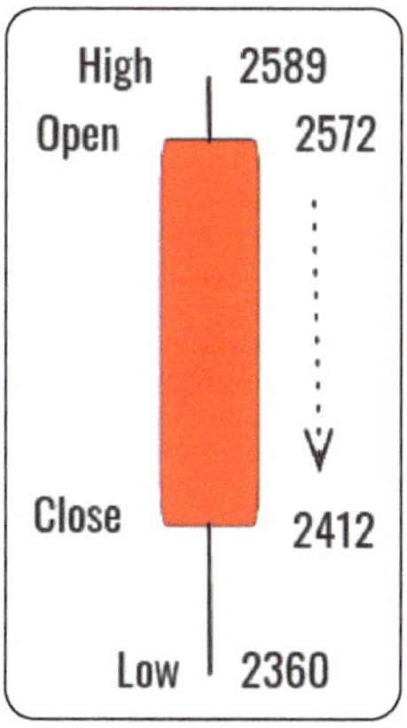

(Fig. 2.6)

This is how the daily timeframe candlestick chart of Reliance Industries Ltd. will look like on the charting platform. (Fig. 2.7):

(Fig. 2.7)

So, as you can see, a great deal of information is available through the candlestick chart in a visually pleasing format. Furthermore, the data points used in the above examples are real & one can confirm it on any charting platform.

Each candlestick provides an easy-to-decipher picture of price action. By seeing the candlestick, a trader can visually compare the relationship between the open-close and the high-low. The association between the open and close is vital and forms the essence of candlesticks.

One cannot ignore the fact that investors' psychologically driven forces of fear, greed, and hope greatly influence stock prices. However, one can track the overall market psychology through candlestick analysis. More than just a pattern recognition method, candlestick analysis shows the interaction between buyers and sellers.

Japanese candlesticks offer a quick picture of the psychology of short-term trading, studying the effect, not the cause. Combining candlestick analysis with other technical analysis tools can be an advantageous way to select entry and exit points.

Takeaways:

- Volume is one of the most crucial elements while doing technical analysis.
- Higher the Volume during a price move, the higher the move's significance. Similarly, the lower the Volume, the lesser the significance of the move.
- Active market participants are the ones who drive the prices.
- A candlestick tells a story of the fight between bulls & bears. Also, in the end, it shows who won the battle.
- Candlesticks and other technical indicators can be fruitful in taking entry & exit decisions.

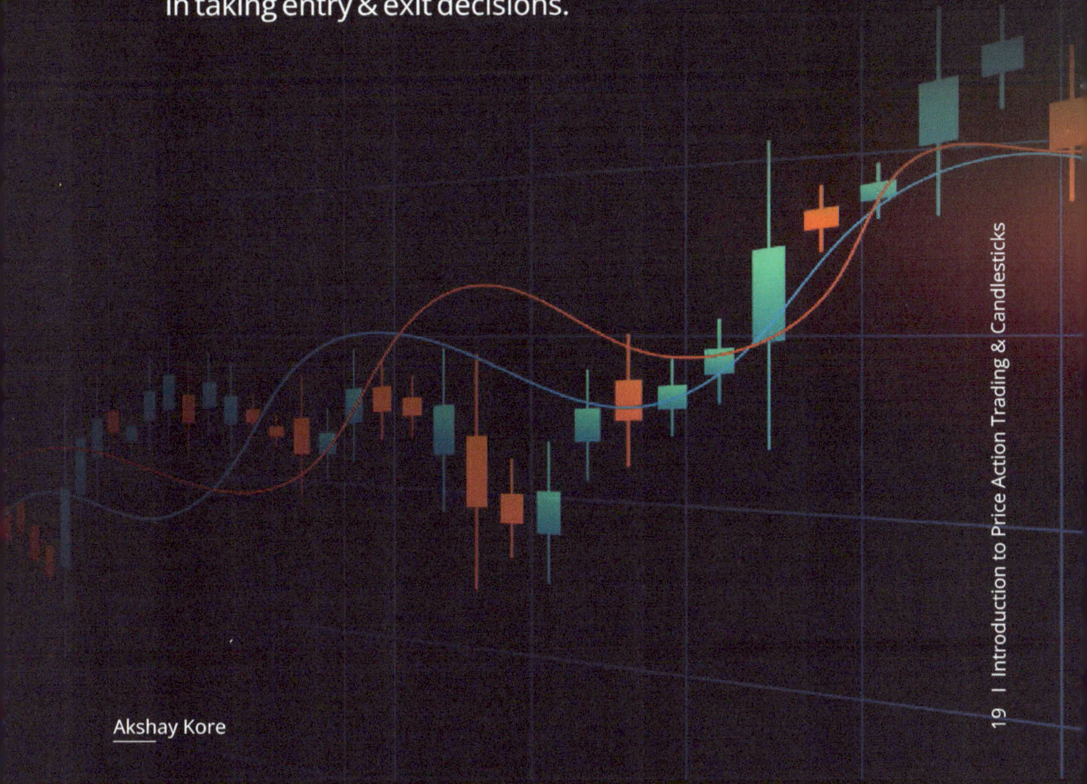

CHAPTER 3
Candlestick Patterns

Now that we have understood how candlesticks form let us know how you can analyze stock prices using these Candlesticks.

There are different candlestick patterns that one needs to know before trading using price action techniques.

Candlestick Patterns :

(**Note:** There are over 30 candlestick patterns that can be learnt & put into practice on actual charts. However, in this book, I have explained those patterns which appear frequently, have a high chance of profitability in the stock market and can be easily spotted on live charts.)

There are essentially two types of candlestick patterns - ***Bullish and Bearish***.

As seen in Fig 3.1, each is further divided based on the number of candlesticks that form a particular pattern.

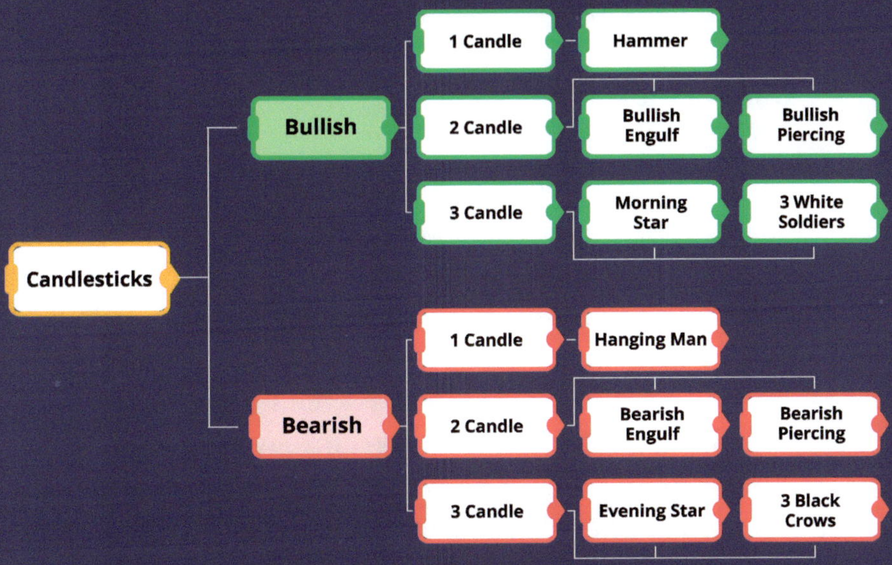
Candlesticks
Bullish
1 Candle
Hammer
2 Candle
Bullish Engulf
Bullish Piercing
3 Candle
Morning Star
3 White Soldiers
Bearish
1 Candle
Hanging Man
2 Candle
Bearish Engulf
Bearish Piercing
3 Candle
Evening Star
3 Black Crows

(Fig. 3.1)

We will begin by understanding all the Bullish patterns first followed by the Bearish patterns.

1. One Candlestick Pattern :

Hammer :

Hammer (Fig 3.2) is a one-candlestick pattern seen in a downtrend when bulls start to step into the rally. It is named so because the candlestick looks like a hammer after being formed completely. The hammer's lower shadow is at least twice the body's length. Although the body's colour is insignificant, a green body has slightly more bullish implications than a red body.

A Hammer pattern forms in the following situation: When the market opens, the sellers are in control, pushing the price lower. However, at the peak of selling, tremendous buying pressure steps in and pushes the price higher. This buying pressure is so intense that the candlestick closes above the opening price.

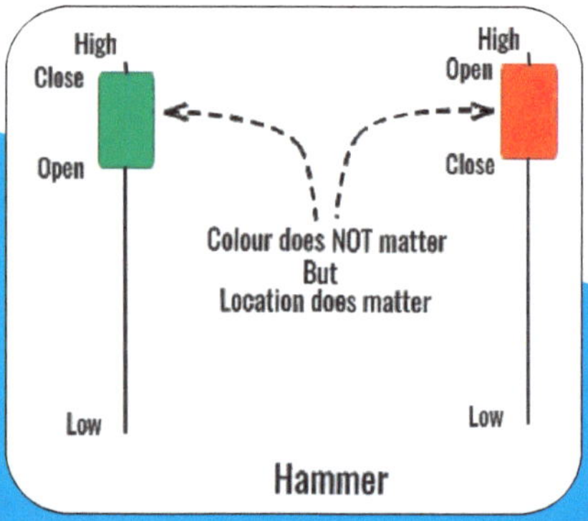

(Fig. 3.2)

Hammer Pattern Identification Checklist :

- The lower shadow = 2 x (the length of the real body).
- The upper shadow should either be absent or very small.
- The real body is always at the upper end of the trading range of the candle
- This pattern has formed after a prolonged or a short downtrend.

Hammer Pattern Trade Setup (Fig 3.3):

- Firstly identify the hammer pattern correctly.
- Large volume on Hammer day increases the chances of price reversal.
- The follow-up candle after the hammer pattern must open above the closing price of the hammer.
- A hammer candle appearing at the support level is considered a high- probability bullish reversal.
- Always remember that there must be a follow-up candle after the hammer pattern to confirm the strength of the buyers.

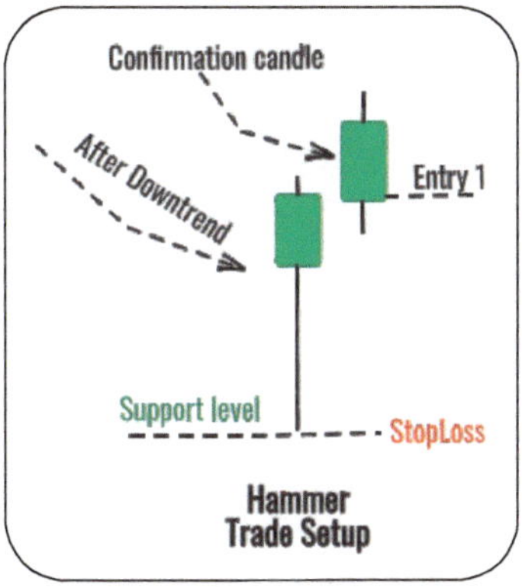

(Fig. 3.3)

To sum up everything, a hammer is a bullish candlestick reversal pattern that shows rejection of lower prices & hence it has to appear after a short downtrend.

Case Study 1: SBI - Daily Time frame - 7th March 2022 (Chart 1). Strong reversal after the Hammer pattern.

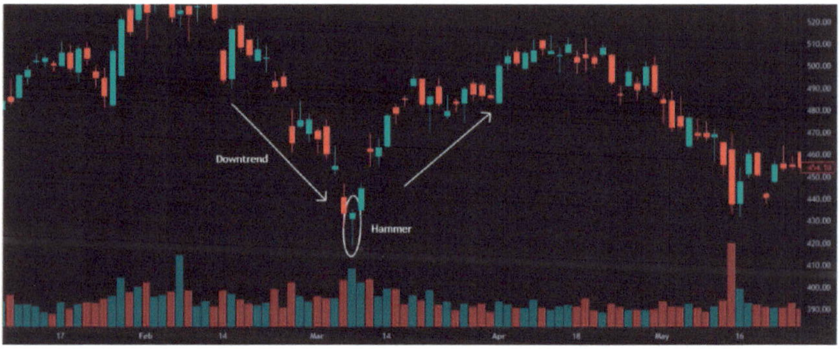

(Chart 1)

Case Study 2: TCS - Daily Time frame - Aug 2021 (Chart 2).

A hammer pattern is seen at a support level & the next corresponding up move is seen.

(Chart 2)

2. Two Candlesticks Pattern :

A) Bullish Engulfing:

A Bullish Engulfing pattern (Fig 3.4) consists of a large green real body that engulfs a small red real body after a downtrend. It signifies that the buyers are overpowering the sellers..

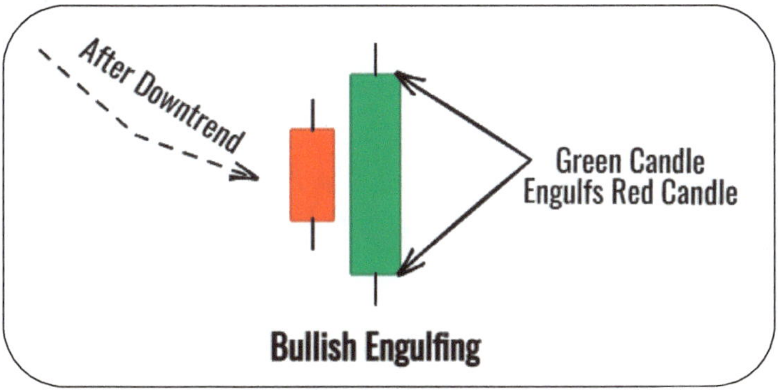

(Fig. 3.4)

The Bullish Engulfing pattern is a significant reversal pattern formed by two opposite-coloured bodies. This Bullish Pattern forms after a downtrend when a small red candlestick is succeeded by a large green candlestick that completely engulfs the candlestick formed the previous day.

It opens lower than the previous day's close and closes higher than the previous day's open.

Bullish Engulfing Pattern Identification Checklist :

- A prolonged or short-term downtrend before this pattern appears.

- The next big green-coloured candle wholly engulfs a small red candle body.
- A large volume on the engulfing day increases the probability that buyers are in full force & ready to take on the sellers.
- Suppose the engulfing body engulfs & absorbs both the body and the shadows of the previous candle. In that case, the reversal has a greater probability of working out.
- There must be a follow-up candle which closes above the close of the previous engulfing green candle.
- Lastly, a Bullish Engulfing pattern appearing at a crucial support level is considered a high-probability bullish reversal.

Bullish Engulfing Pattern Trade Setup (Fig 3.5):

- Firstly identify the Bullish Engulf pattern correctly.
- Since this pattern consists of 2 candlesticks, it is formed entirely on the second day at the close.
- Aggressive Traders can enter at the end of second day just before the market closes, as, by that time, it is understood that a Bullish Engulfing pattern is formed.
- Conservative traders can enter the next day once the bullish confirmation candle forms.ie. on the third day. Though this would be a late entry and you will have to pay more premium, your conviction while taking that position will be stronger.
- The stop loss for both the traders would be the lowest low point of both the candles.

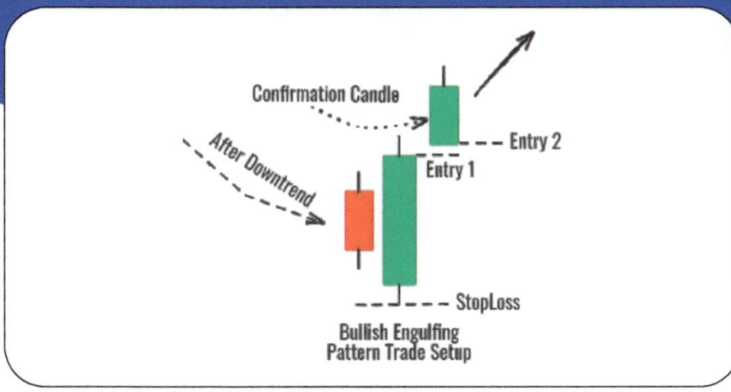

(Fig. 3.5)

Case Study 3: Reliance Industries - Daily Timeframe - 29th September 2022 (Chart 3). A strong reversal is seen right after the engulfing pattern at the support level.

(Chart 3)

Case Study 4: SBI - Daily Timeframe - 11th March 2020 (Chart 4). No follow-up candle to the pattern & it fails.
So here, if you had waited for the next day after the pattern was formed, there would have been no entry at all since no confirmation candle could be seen.
So do remember, ***no pattern works 100% of the time.***

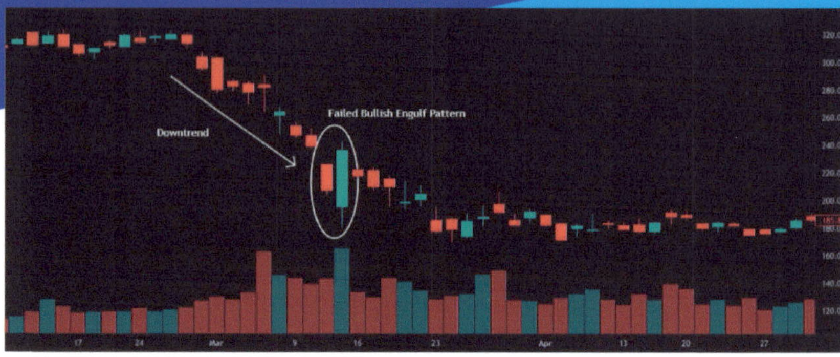

(Chart 4)

Case Study 5: Voltas Ltd - Daily Timeframe - Aug 2021(Chart 5). It can be seen that a bullish engulfing candle has engulfed 3 - 4 previous red candles & you can see how significant the next uptrend was.

(Chart 5)

B) Bullish Piercing:

This piercing pattern (Fig 3.6) is similar to the bullish engulfing pattern with a minor variation. It is composed of a two-candle formation in a down-trending market and will often end a minor downtrend.

Now, when I say minor trend, it simply means a downtrend that lasts anywhere between 4 to 15 days.

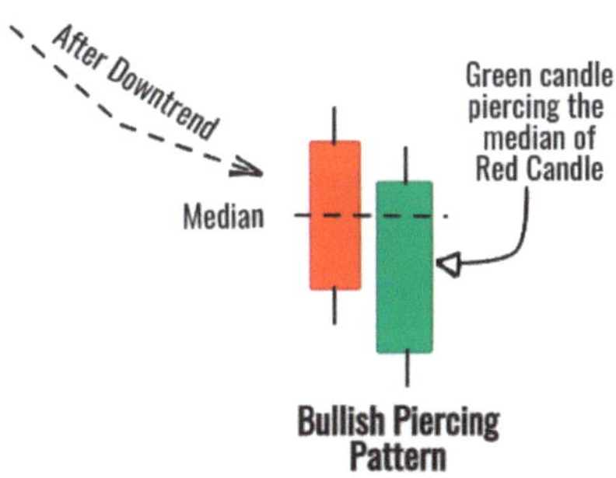

(Fig. 3.6)

As you see in this image, the day before the piercing candle appears, the daily candle should be a large body red candle showing the aggression of sellers.

Bullish Piercing Pattern Identification Checklist:

- The prior downtrend should last for at least 4 to 15 days.
- The body of the 1st candle is big red & the body of the immediate next candle is green.
- The green candle closes above the median of the previous red candle.

- The green candle opens below the close of the previous red candle.
- A Bullish piercing pattern appearing at the support level is considered strong bullish.

Bullish Piercing Pattern Trade Setup (Fig 3.7):

- Identify the Bullish Piercing pattern correctly.
- Again, since this pattern consists of 2 candlesticks, it is completely formed on the second day at close
- The entry rules will be the same as that of the Bullish Engulfing pattern
- The stop loss for both the traders would be the Lowest Low point of both the candles.

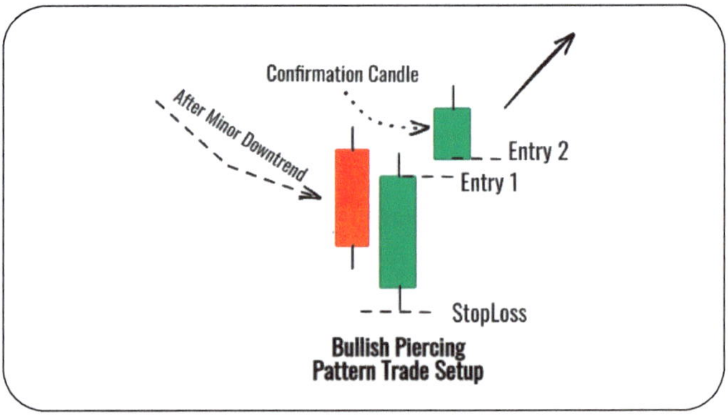

(Fig. 3.7)

Case Study 6: Escorts Ltd - Daily Timeframe - 22nd August 2022 (Chart 6).

A strong reversal right after the Bullish Piercing pattern.

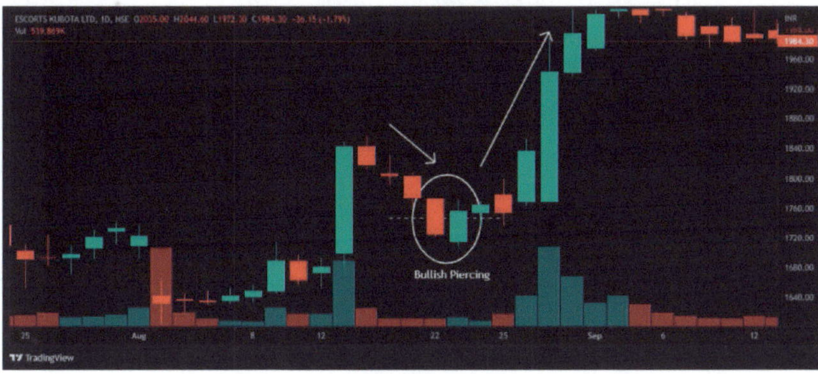

(Chart 6)

Case Study 7: Escorts Ltd - Daily Timeframe - 29th March 2022 (Chart 7).

A strong reversal right after the Bullish Piercing pattern.

The piercing green candle has, however, closed precisely at the median of the red candle.

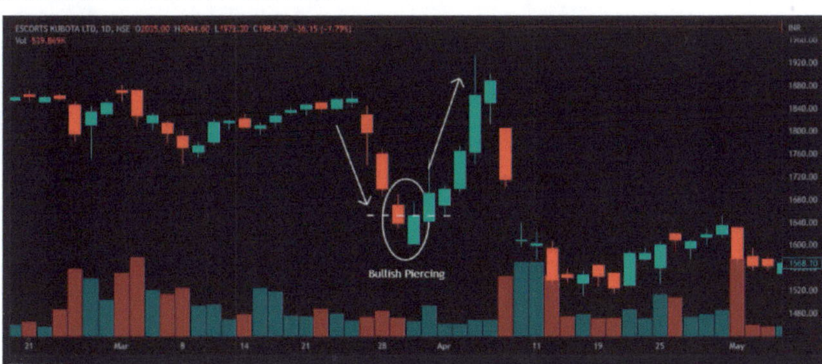

(Chart 7)

Case Study 8 : Amara Raja Batteries - Daily Timeframe - 26th August 2021(Chart 8)

(Chart 8)

Case Study 9: Manappuram Finance Ltd.- Monthly Timeframe - 1st June 2022 (Chart 9).

(Chart 9)

2. Three Candlestick Pattern

A) Morning Star :

A Morning Star (Fig 3.8) is a three candlestick bullish reversal pattern which appears at the bottom of a downtrend.

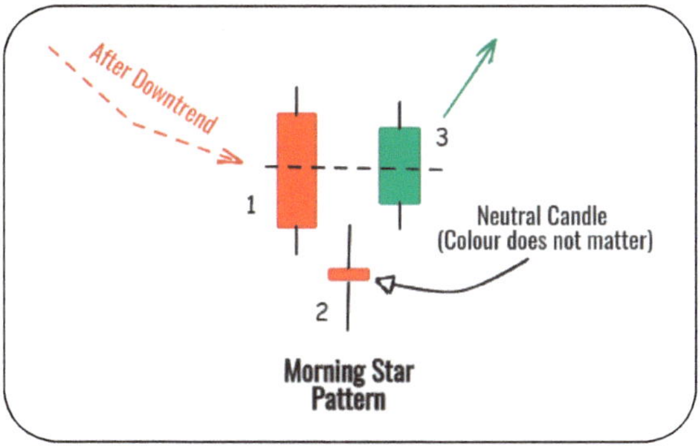

(Fig. 3.8)

As you see in this image, the 3rd green candle closes above the median of the 1st red candle.

Morning Star Pattern Identification Checklist:

- There must be a prior downtrend & the market is continuously making new Lows during this period.
- The body of the 1st candle is red, as per the downtrend. The second candle formed is a Doji (or an indecisive candle).
- The 3rd candle is green in colour & has crossed the median of the 1st red candle. Crossing the median point is the most critical aspect of this pattern.
- This pattern appearing at a support level increases the bullishness of the trade.

Morning Star Pattern Trade Setup (Fig 3.9):

- The entry will be on the 3rd candle at close for aggressive traders, provided the closing point is above the median of the 1st red candle.
- Conservative traders may enter late on the following day if the price opens above the close of the 3rd candle.
- Both traders will have stoploss at the lowest point of the pattern.

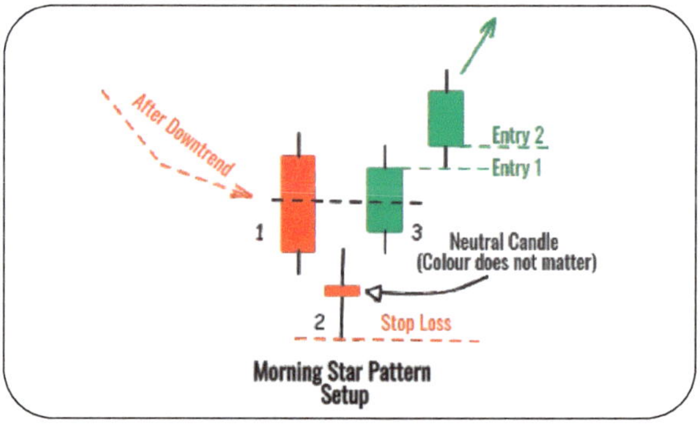

(Fig. 3.9)

Case Study 10: Ashok Leyland - Daily Time Frame - 7th March 2022 (Chart 10).

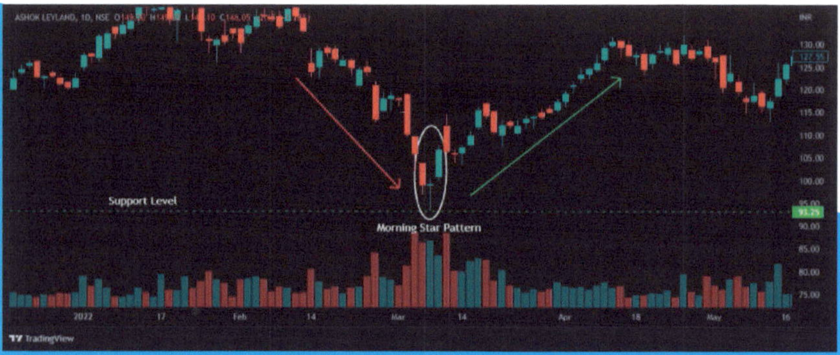

(Chart 10)

Case Study 11: State Bank of India - Daily Timeframe - 20th August 2021 (Chart 11).

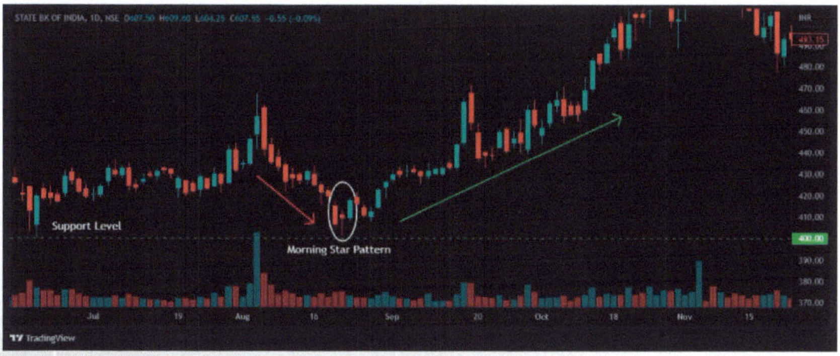

(Chart 11)

B) Three White Soldiers:

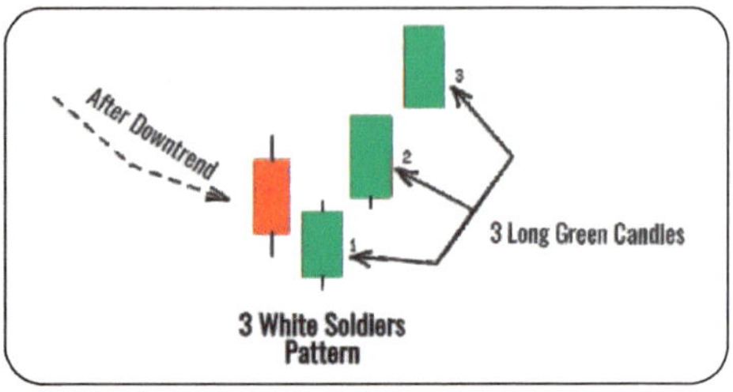

(Fig 3.10)

Three white soldiers (Fig 3.10) is another bullish candlestick pattern used to predict the reversal after a short-term or a long-term downtrend.

This pattern is also known as the Three Advancing White Soldiers. It forms after a long downtrend when the bullish forces exceed the bearish forces for three consecutive candles. This pattern will be primarily visible on intraday timeframes such as 5 min, 15 min or 1 hr. However, this pattern may appear on the daily timeframe also when buying is too strong.

Three White Soldiers Pattern Identification Checklist:

- The pattern will generally be formed after a prolonged downtrend or a sideways trend.
- The body of the 1st candle will be big & green in colour, with little or no wicks showing good strength of the buyers.
- The following 2nd candle will also be green in colour & of the same size or even bigger than the first one. Again it will have little or no wicks at all.
- The 3rd consecutive candle will also be green in colour with a huge size, showing that the buyers are ready to pay any premium to enter the trade. To sum up, all three green candles will be very similar in size.
- All three green candles may have little or no wicks at all, but the size of the real body must match.

3 White Soldiers Pattern Trade Setup (Fig 3.11):

- The entry must be taken on the 3rd candle at closing for aggressive traders & on the 4th candle at open if you are a conservative trader.
- Once the three candles are formed, a retracement may be seen up to the median point of the 2nd candle.
- One can also add more quantity during the retracement period. However, like always, the retracement is not guaranteed.
- Since the retracement is not guaranteed, one has to enter at the opening price of the following candles because if the candle turns out green by closing, you would have lost an opportunity to buy at a lower premium.
- The stoploss will be the lowest point of the pattern.

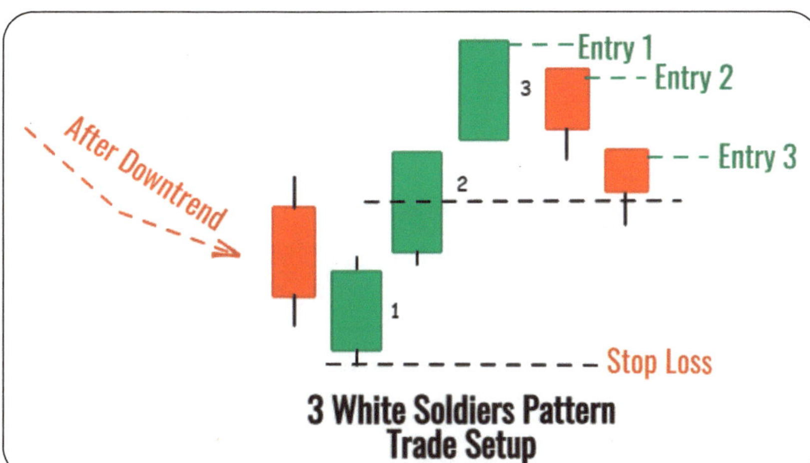

(Fig. 3.11)

Case Study 12: Bank Of India - Weekly Timeframe - 24th October 2022 (Chart 12).In this chart, you can see a prolonged sideways trend before 3 White Soldiers.

(Chart 12)

Case Study 13: HDFC - Weekly Timeframe - 17th February 2014(Chart 13).

Note that if the 3 White soldiers pattern appears in the Weekly timeframe, it is a clear indication of the buyers' strong dominance of the buyers & the resulting upmove could be very big.

(Chart 13)

1. One Candlestick Pattern :

A) The Hanging Man :

The Hanging man (Fig 3.12) is a bearish reversal candlestick pattern with a small real body, no wick, and a long lower shadow.

It forms when the bulls have pushed the prices up, and now they cannot push further.

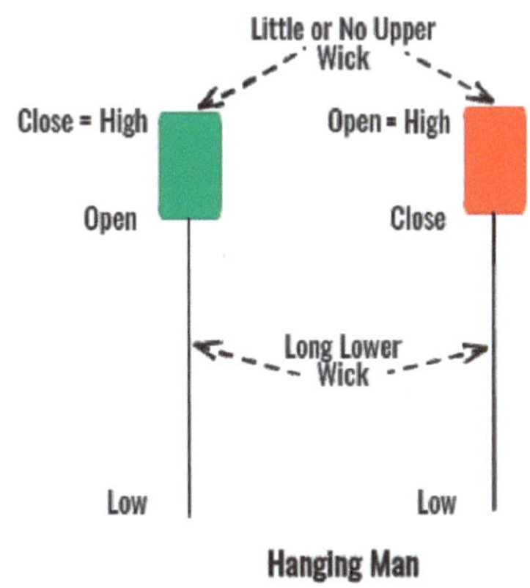

(Fig. 3.12)

This candlestick chart pattern has a small real body, meaning the distance between the opening and closing price is significantly less. There is no upper shadow, and the lower shadow is twice the length of its body.

This pattern allows traders to exit their buy position and enter a short position.

The hanging man candlestick pattern is just a warning signal. For it to be a valid reversal pattern, the price must move lower down on the next candle. This is called confirmation.

Hanging Man Pattern Identification checklist:

- Market is in an uptrend before the formation of the hanging man.

- The real body is tiny and located at the candlestick's upper end.
- It has a very long lower wick (2-3 times the size of the real body) & no upper wick, as seen in the above image. If the upper wick is present, it should be tiny.
- Its colour can be red or green. However, the red body is more bearish.
- A hanging man appearing at a critical resistance level is considered a high probability bearish reversal.

Hanging Man Pattern Trade Setup (Fig 3.13):

- The entry must be taken the day after the hanging man pattern is completely formed.
- The stop loss will be the highpoint of the Hanging man.
- Suppose there is a Gap-up the next day after the formation of the Hanging man. In that case, it is not a valid hanging man & one should refrain from taking any trade in such a scenario.
- As mentioned earlier, a Hanging man with a red body formed at a resistance level has a high probability of winning.

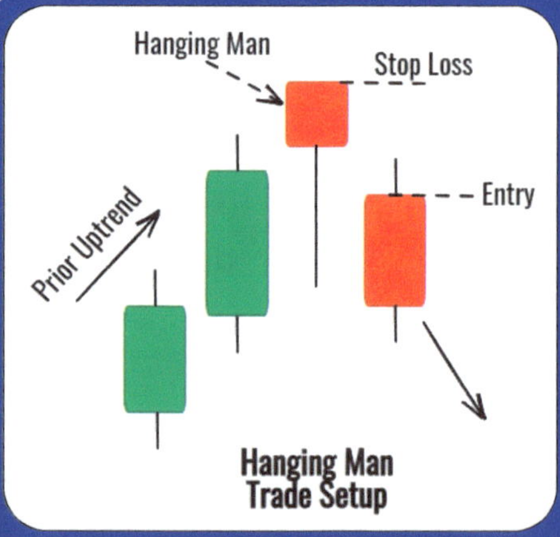

(Fig. 3.13)

Case Study 14: Silver Futures Chart Daily Timeframe - Oct 2022 (Chart 14).

You can see the hanging man being formed at a resistance level.

(Chart 14)

Case Study 15: Hero Moto Corp. - Daily Timeframe - 17th September 2021 (Chart 15).

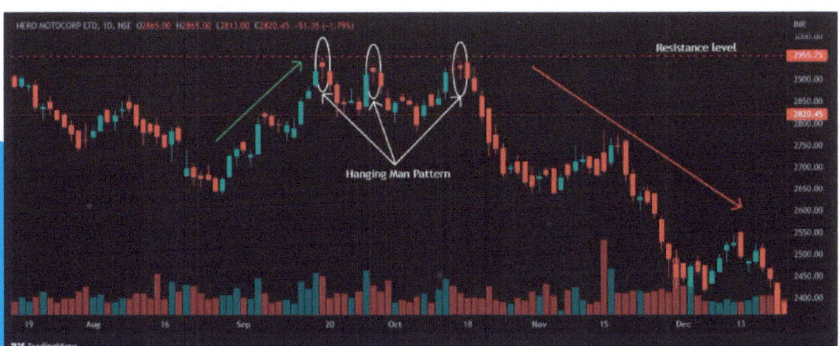

(Chart 15)

Case Study 16: HCL Tech Ltd. - Daily Timeframe - 12th January 2022. (Chart 16).

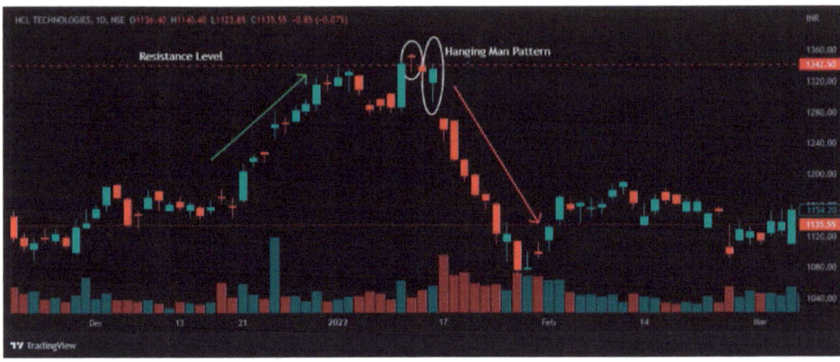

(Chart 16)

B) Bearish Engulfing:

A Bearish Engulfing pattern (Fig 3.14) forms when a small green real body is engulfed by a large red real body after an uptrend. It signifies that the sellers are overpowering the buyers.

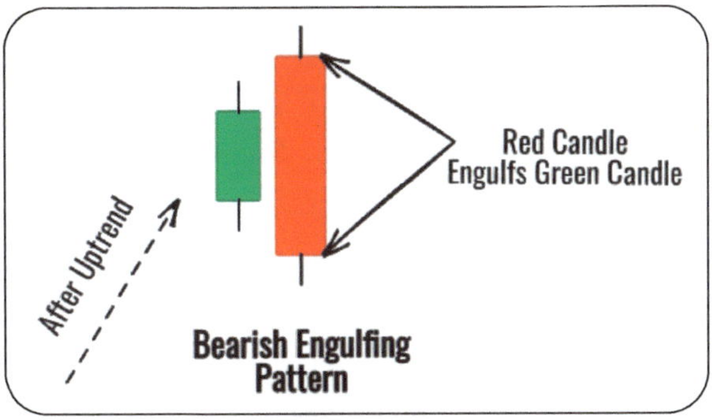

(Fig. 3.14)

It is a major reversal pattern formed by two opposite-coloured bodies. This Bearish Pattern forms after an uptrend. It is formed when the 1st small green candlestick is followed by a 2nd large red candlestick that completely engulfs the 1st candlestick.

The 2nd red candle opens higher than the previous green candle's close and closes lower than the previous green candle's open.

Bearish Engulfing Pattern Identification Checklist:

- There is a prolonged or a short-term uptrend before this pattern appears.
- A small green candle body is the 1st candle in this pattern.

- The next candle generally opens with a gap up(signifying a bullish signal). However, the dominant bears drive the price further down to close the candle below the opening of the previous green-bodied candle.
- Visually it can be seen that the 2nd big red candle completely engulfs the 1st green candle.
- Large selling volume on the engulfing day increases the probability that sellers are in full force & ready to take on the buyers.
- Suppose that the engulfing body engulfs & absorbs both the body and the shadows of the previous candle. In that case, the reversal has a greater probability of working out.
- There must be a follow-up candle that opens below the close of the big red candle.
- Lastly, a Bearish Engulfing pattern appearing at the critical resistance level is considered a high probability bearish reversal.

Bearish Engulf Pattern Trade Setup (Fig 3.15):

- Since this pattern consists of 2 candlesticks, its formation is completed only once the second candle formation is done.
- Aggressive Traders can enter at the end of 2nd day just before the market closes, as, by that time, it is understood that a Bearish Engulfing pattern is formed.
- Conservative traders can enter the next day once the price opens below the close of the Big red candle. However, it will be a late entry, and you will sell at a much lower level. Still, again you would also be more confident while taking that position.

- The stoploss for both conservative and aggressive traders would be the highest point of both the candles

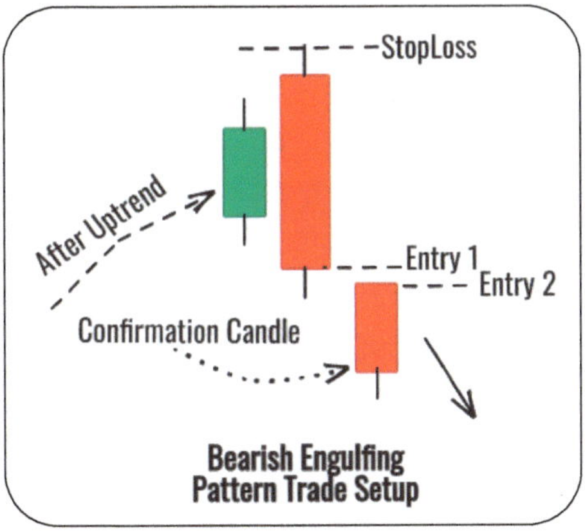

(Fig. 3.15)

Case Study 17: TCS - Daily Timeframe 21/06/2021 (Chart 17). It can be seen in the chart that a bearish engulfing pattern is formed at the resistance level. In the same chart, a bullish hammer pattern is also seen at support levels.

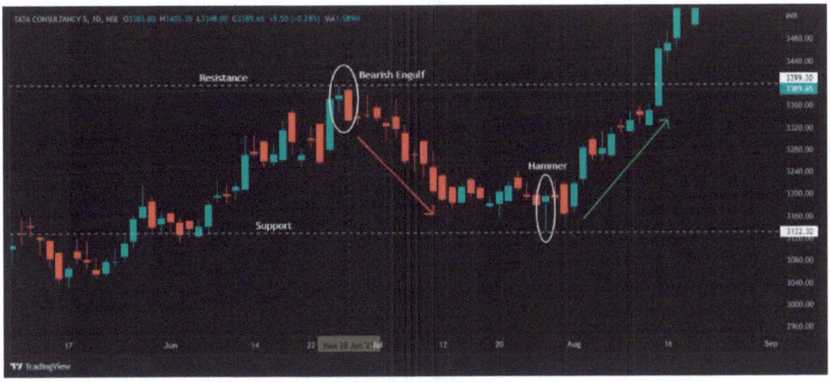

(Chart 17)

Case Study 18: Gold Futures - Daily Timeframe - June 2021 (Chart 18).

Here the big red candle engulfs the previous candles & this shows the massive strength of the sellers, which pushes the prices down afterwards.

(Chart 18)

Case Study 19: Gold Futures - Daily Timeframe - August 2020 (Chart 19).

Here again, the big red candle engulfs the previous two candles & you can see what has happened next.

(Chart 19)

Case Study 20: Bank Nifty - Daily Timeframe - 31st May 2022 (Chart 20).

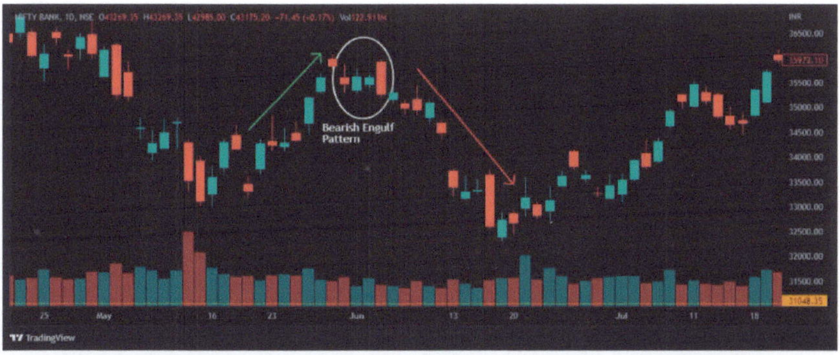

(Chart 20)

B) Bearish Piercing:

The piercing pattern (Fig 3.16) is remarkably similar to the bearish engulfing pattern with a minor variation. It is composed of a two-candle formation in an up-trending market and will often end with a minor uptrend.

When I say minor trend, it simply means an uptrend that lasts anywhere between 4 to 15 days.

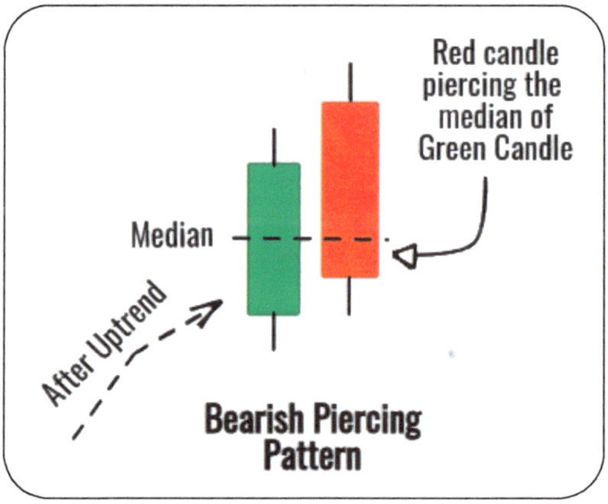

(Fig. 3.16)

As you see in the above image, the day before the piercing red candle appears, the daily candle should be a large green candle showing the aggression of buyers.

Bearish Piercing Pattern Identification Checklist:

- ✓ The prior uptrend should at least last for a period of 4 to 15 days.
- ✓ The body of the first candle is big & green in colour & the body of the immediate next candle is red.

- The 2nd red candle closes below the median of the 1st green candle.
- A Bearish piercing pattern appearing at the resistance level is considered more bearish.

Bearish Piercing Pattern Trade Setup (Fig 3.17):

- Since this pattern consists of 2 candlesticks, it is entirely formed on the second day at the close.
- The entry rules will be the same as that of the Bearish Engulfing pattern, as shown in the image.
- The stop loss for both the traders would be the highest point of both the candles.

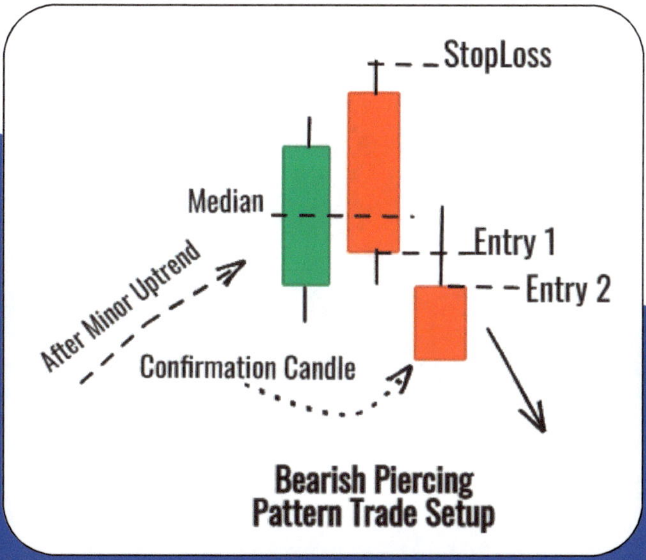

(Fig. 3.17)

Case Study 21: Gokaldas Exports - Daily Timeframe - 14th July 2021 (Chart 21).

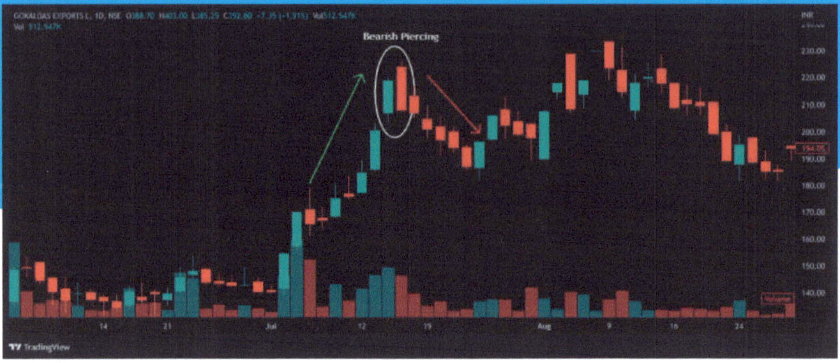

(Chart 21)

Case Study 22: Amara Raja Batteries - Daily Timeframe - 17th January 2022 (Chart 22).

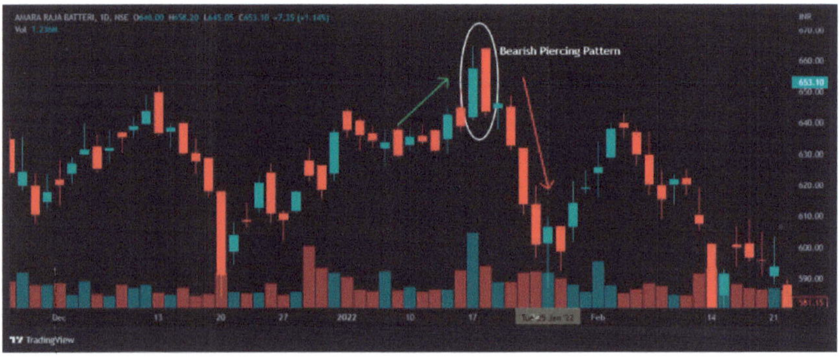

(Chart 22)

3. Three candlesticks pattern

A) Evening Star Pattern:

An Evening Star (Fig 3.18) is a 3-candle bearish reversal pattern that generally appears at the top of an uptrend

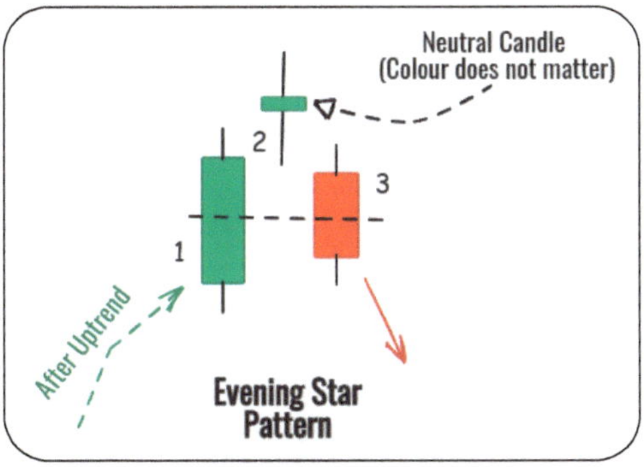

(Fig. 3.18)

As you can see, the third red candle closes below the median of the 1st green candle.

Evening Star Pattern Identification Checklist:

- There must be a prior uptrend & the market is continuously making new Highs during this period.
- The 1st candle's body is green, as per the uptrend. The 2nd candle formed is a Doji (or an indecisive candle).
- The 3rd candle is red & has crossed the median of the 1st green candle. Crossing & closing below the median point is the most critical aspect of this pattern.
- This pattern appearing at a resistance level further increases the bearishness of the trade.

Evening Star Pattern Trade Setup (Fig 3.19):

- The entry will be on the 3rd candle at close for aggressive traders, provided the closing point is below the median of the 1st green candle.
- Conservative traders may enter late, at the next candle, if the price opens below the close of the 3rd candle, as shown in the image.
- Both traders will have stop loss at the Highest point of the pattern.

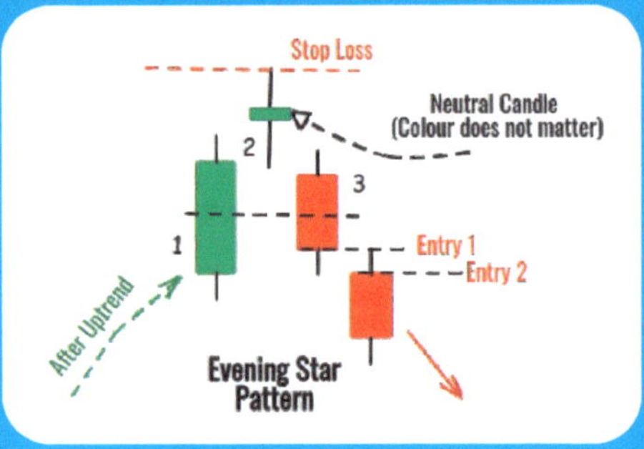

(Fig. 3.19)

Case Study 23: Amara Raja Batteries - Daily Timeframe - 1st February 2022 (Chart 23).

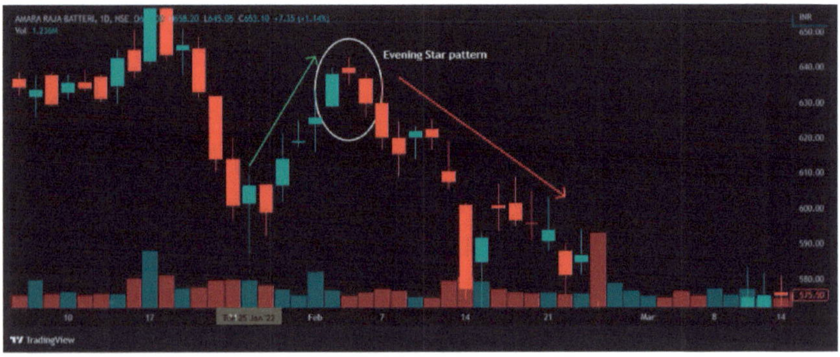

(Chart 23)

Case Study 24: Kotak Mahindra Bank - Daily Timeframe - 9th March 2021 (Chart 24).

(Chart 24)

B) Three Black Crows:

Three Black Crows pattern (Fig 3.20) predicts reversal after a short-term or a long-term uptrend. It is a bearish candlestick pattern.

It's the opposite of Three White Soldiers. It is formed after a long uptrend when the bearish forces exceed the bullish forces for three consecutive days.

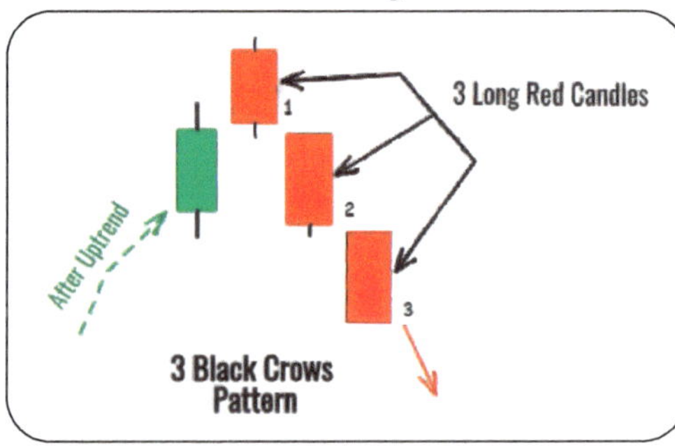

(Fig. 3.20)

Three Black Crows Pattern Identification Checklist:

- The pattern will be formed after a prolonged uptrend. It may also be seen in an ongoing downtrend.
- The body of the first candle will be big red, with little or no wicks showing the excellent strength of the sellers.
- The following candle will also be red & of the same size or even bigger than the first one. Again it will have little or no wicks at all.
- The third consecutive candle will also be red with a huge size, showing that the sellers are ready to pay any premium to enter the trade. To sum up, all three red candles will be very similar in size.
- Note that all three red candles will have little or no wicks.

Three Black Crows Pattern Trade Setup (Fig 3.21):

- If you are an aggressive trader, the entry must be taken on the 3rd candle at closing & if you are a conservative trader, on the 4th day at the opening.
- Once the three candles are formed, retracement may be seen up to the median point of the 2nd candle in the coming days.
- One can also add more quantity during the retracement period. However, like always, the retracement is not guaranteed.
- Since the retracement is not guaranteed, one has to enter at the opening price of the following candles because you may never know; the candle may turn out red by closing & you would have lost an opportunity to sell at a higher price.
- The stop loss will be the highest point of the pattern.

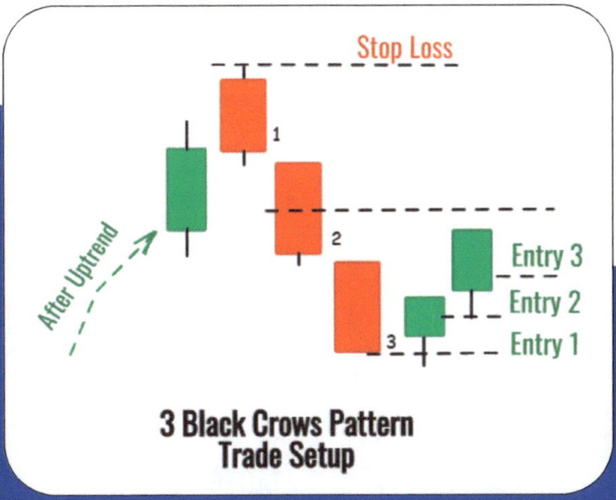

(Fig. 3.21)

Case Study 25 : Silver Futures - 1 Hr Timeframe - 26th September, 2022

A classic Three Black crows pattern seen here (Chart 25). You can see a pullback/retracement till the median of the central red candle, where short entry can be taken as per the setup.

(Chart 25)

Case Study 26: HCL Tech - 1Hr Timeframe - 11th July 2022 (Chart 26).

Note that this pattern may also be seen in an ongoing downtrend, as seen in the below chart.

(Chart 26)

Case Study 27: Paytm - 15 min Timeframe - 9th November 2022 (Chart 27).

Remember that this pattern will most probably be seen in shorter timeframes.

(Chart 27)

Case Study 28: Nifty Intraday - 5 min Timeframe - 2nd December 2022. (Chart 28).

(Chart 28)

CHAPTER 4
Support & Resistance

Support & Resistance :

Support & Resistance are critical levels where the forces of supply & demand meet. Therefore, these supports and resistances are essential for Technical analysts while taking any trade positions.

In layperson's terms,

Support levels are levels where the *stock demand* is strong, preventing the stock price from falling deeper.

Resistance levels are levels where the *supply is strong enough*, restricting the stock price from moving upwards.

Check out Fig 4.1. You can see the supply & demand zone plotted on the Reliance Industries chart.

(Fig 4.1)

(On a side note, drawing from our knowledge about candlesticks from the previous chapter, you can see that a Bearish Engulfing pattern has formed at the resistance level, and a hammer pattern is formed at the support level.)

Now, let us understand how demand and supply zones are formed and the market psychology behind them.

Let's assume that there are buyers who are buying some XYZ stock close to a support area & let us say that the support level is Rs. 300/-. So now they buy this stock at Rs 300/- & the price moves up to Rs. 330/-. The buyers are now happy & want to buy more quantities of the same stock , but at Rs. 300/- only and not at Rs 330/-. So they cumulatively decide to buy the stock only if the price moves back to Rs 300/-. As a result, a demand zone is created at the 300 level. *This is how the demand zone is formed.*

Suppose another group of investors considered purchasing the stock when it was Rs. 300/-. However, they could not enter the stock at the said price for unavoidable reasons. Now the stock has reached Rs. 330/- and they regret not buying it when it was at Rs.300/-. So they decide that if the stock falls back to Rs.300/- they will not repeat the same mistake & buy the stock this time. This further creates potential demand.

Another group of investors entered the same stock at Rs.270/-. However, they exited once the price reached Rs.300/- , only to watch it go to Rs.330/-. So now they regret selling the stock & want to re-establish their long position again & want to repurchase it at the same price they sold it, ie. Rs.300/-.

So basically, they have changed their overall sentiment from sellers to buyers. So again, a demand is created.

On similar grounds, let us understand how a *supply zone forms.*

In the assumption mentioned earlier, suppose that all the investors hold a stock XYZ for Rs.300/. Now the stock goes to Rs.370 in quick time, which is a return of almost 23%. However, the investors felt that it would further move up & they did not book any profit at the Rs.370/- level. Now the stock takes a U-turn & is again back to the Rs.300/- level. Now, what are your feelings? First, you regret not selling at Rs.370/- with a 23% profit. Now assume that the stock reached Rs.370/- again & this time, you exited all your positions with good profits.

This is also done by other investors who missed the earlier opportunity to exit. Many other stock owners are trying to square off their positions this time. This creates a resistance level at Rs.370/-.

I hope things are clearly understood now. These are only a few examples of several likely scenarios. If you have traded before, you have probably been through all these scenarios and experienced the sentiments and psychology behind them. However, do remember that you are not alone. Countless market participants are going through the same feelings and thought processes as you are, and this is what helps establish some of the market psychology behind support - resistance and Technical analysis in general.

Remember that :

Technical analysis is 80% Psychological & 20% Logical.
Fundamental analysis is 80% Logical & 20% Psychological.

A principle Technical analysis concept is that *when a resistance or support level is broken, a role reversal occurs at that very moment*. If the price falls below the support level, that particular level will immediately become the resistance level. If the price goes (rises) above a resistance level, that level will often turn into support. As the price passes a support or resistance level, it is thought that supply and demand have shifted, causing the breached level to reverse its role.

To conclude, remember that technical analysis is not a precise science and depends on personal interpretation. As you continue your study of technical analysis, you are likely to hear someone say that it is a science and art. As with any other discipline, it takes commitment and hard work to become adept at it!

Plotting Of Supports & Resistance on Chart :

Before we learn how to plot support and resistance levels on any chart, one must always keep in mind that:

- To identify short-term support & resistance, you must load at least 4 to 6 months of data.
- If you want to identify long-term support & resistance, load at least 12 to 15 months of data points.
- Long-term support & resistance – Used for swing trading.
- Short-term support & resistance – Used for intraday and short-term trades.

Steps for Plotting Support & Resistance :

Step 1: First, load the data using appropriate timeframes: Daily, Weekly or Monthly. Let's understand all this with an example. So let us load the data by selecting the weekly timeframe of the stock - Reliance Industries Ltd.

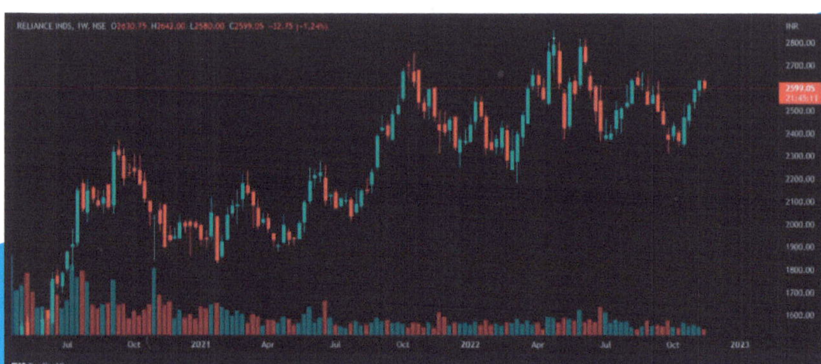

(Step 1)

So this is what we get - data ranging from July 2020 to October 2022. Our intention here is to find the long-term support & resistance of Reliance Industries Ltd.

Step 2: Circle all the tops & bottoms seen in the chart.

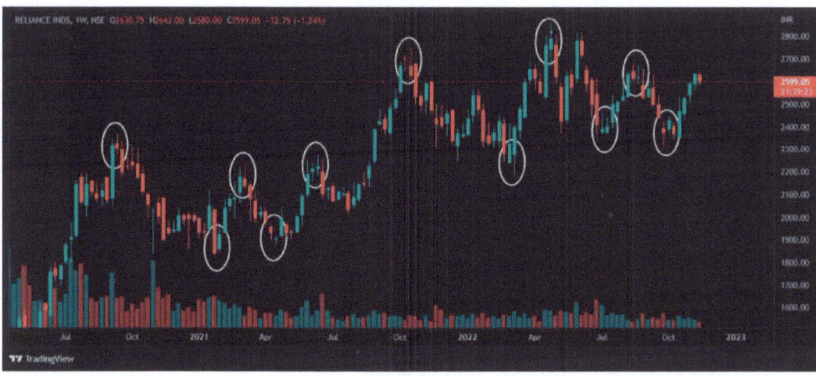

(Step 2)

Step 3: Try & connect all the tops & all the bottoms. Once connected, your chart will look something like this, as shown in the image below.

(Step 3)

While connecting the circles, you will accommodate the maximum points on the drawn line. You may prefer touching the line to the candle's body rather than the wick. Try to connect at least three data points while drawing the support line.

Step 4: Now remove all the circles on the chart to remove unnecessary clutter.

(Step 4)

You can see that, somehow, these horizontal lines & trend lines drawn in white have been respected during the entire time frame.

So by now, you must have understood that Reliance Industries Limited is currently at a resistance level & you can also see a small red candle being formed at the end step 5.

(Step 5)

You can now analyze things better by comparing the chart in step 5 with the chart shown in step 1. Since Reliance is now at a resistance level, it may not be a good idea to buy the stock at this stage. However, note that a resistance level, once broken by price action with huge volumes, will behave like a support in the future.

So in the stated example, if the current resistance level of 2700/- is broken, it will behave like a support level for upcoming days.

Trendlines:

Trendline (also known as *dynamic resistance & support*) is another important technical analysis tool.

Trendlines are drawn on charts by connecting a series of price points. The resulting line indicates the direction in which the stock might move. They also reveal the strength of the trend. Steeper trendlines show more momentum than less steep ones.

How to draw a trendline?

To draw a trendline, we need at least two touchpoints. One has to join the two initial points & then extend the line to know the probable path of the price in future. Having more touchpoints offer validity & solidarity to the trendline.

More precisely, a trendline can be drawn on the price charts by joining all the lows in the uptrend and all the peaks in the downtrend.

Example: The white coloured lines drawn on the chart (Fig 4.2) are called Trendlines.

(Fig. 4.2)

What is a Trend Breakout?

A breakout is a move outside of a defined support or resistance area. Breakouts can occur on any timeframe but commonly appear on daily charts (Fig 4.3).

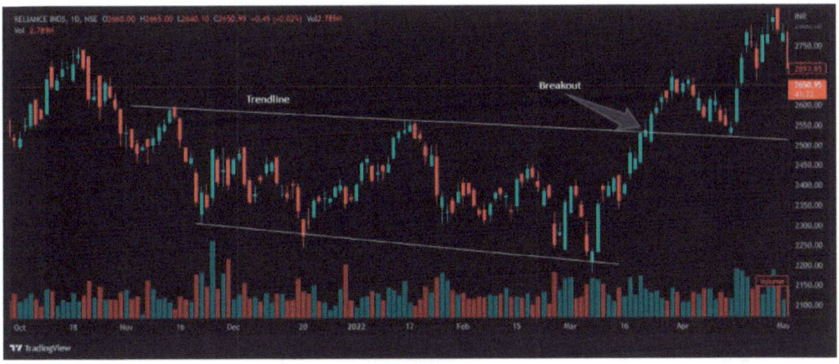

(Fig. 4.3)

Trading a Breakout:

The key to trading breakouts is to wait for a confirmed move outside of support or resistance. This means that the price has closed (or at least reached) a level outside of support or resistance. Once a breakout has been confirmed, the next step is to enter a trade in the direction of the breakout. This can be done by buying or selling at the market price or placing a pending order outside the support or resistance level. Stop losses should be placed just below the previous support or resistance level. This will help to protect against a false breakout.

How to book profits when trading a Trend Breakout :

While trading on a trend breakout, profits can be booked in two ways:

- One popular method is to set a profit level at a Fibonacci retracement level.
- Another approach is to use a multiple of the risk amount.

Breakouts can be a great way to enter a trend. By waiting for a confirmed move and placing a stop loss just below the previous level, traders can limit their risk while still giving themselves a good chance of profiting from the move.

Takeaways:

- Support and Resistance (S&R) levels are key areas where the price of a stock may experience difficulty rising above or falling below.
- S&R levels are used by traders and investors to determine entry and exit points for trades.
- After a breakout has occurred at resistance level, there is a high probability that the original resistance will be retested once by the price.
- On similar grounds, if there is a breakdown at support level, there is a high probability that the original support level will be retested once

CHAPTER 5
Stock Market Phases Every Trader Must Know

The stock market is divided into different phases, each characterized by its unique characteristics and behaviors. These phases include

1. The Bull market
2. The Bear market, and
3. The Sideways market.

The Bull market is characterized by a *general upward trend in stock prices*, as investors are confident and willing to pay higher asset prices. This can lead to increased economic activity and growth as businesses have access to more capital to invest and expand.

On the other hand, a Bear market is typically characterized by a *significant decline in stock prices or index, usually 20% or more from their recent highs*. This can happen when investors become pessimistic about the economy and are less willing to pay high asset prices. This can lead to decreased economic activity and lower growth.

The Sideways market, also known as a range-bound market, is characterized by a lack of clear direction in stock prices. In this phase, stock prices may fluctuate within a relatively narrow range without a clear trend, either up or down. This creates doubt in investors' minds to make decisions, as it is unclear which direction the market is heading.

Overall, the stock market's different phases can significantly impact the economy and individual investors. Therefore, investors must understand these phases and prepare for the potential changes that can occur in the market.

Irrespective of whether the stock market is Bear, Bull or Sideways, it goes through four stages:

1. Accumulation stage
2. Markup Stage or Run-up phase
3. Distribution Stage
4. Markdown Stage

Look at Fig 5.1 to understand these four stages clearly.

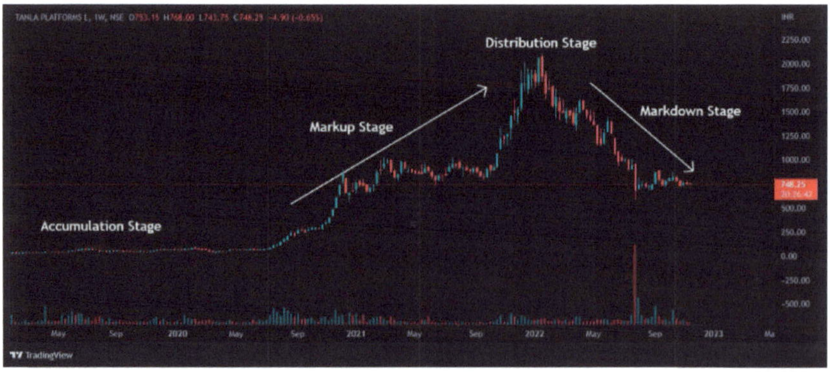

(Fig. 5.1)

Let's understand each of these stages in detail.

1. **Accumulation stage:**
   This stock market phase can be applied to an individual stock or the index as a whole. The accumulation stage has a *vague or unclear trend*. It is a period of pure consolidation spread over a few months to a few years. One would see no increment in the investment made during this phase. During this phase, stock prices may be low, and investors may see value in buying undervalued stocks. As more and more investors start to buy, the demand for stocks increases, pushing prices higher and signaling a new uptrend.

2. **Markup Stage :**
   This phase, also called the run-up phase, shows *rapid movement in prices & new highs are made in no time.* Ideally, one should enter a trade during this phase.
   The run-up phase is a period during which stock prices rise rapidly. This rapid price rise is typically caused by increased demand for stocks, often fueled by positive news or developments within the company or the broader economy. In addition, during the run-up stage, investors may become more hopeful about the future prospects of the companies whose stocks they buy, leading to even more buying and further price increases.

The run-up stage can be a good time for investors to profit by selling their stocks, as prices are likely to be high. However, it's essential to be cautious during this phase, as sharp declines can sometimes follow rapid price increases.

3. **Distribution Stage:**

   This phase is also known as the reversal stage, where traders who purchase stocks during the accumulation phase begin to exit the market. A notable feature of this stage is that *the share volume increases, but the price remains the same.* The market seems bullish, but the demand does not exceed the supply of shares.

   The distribution stage is a period during which stock prices decline. A decrease in stock demand typically causes this, often fueled by negative news or developments within the company or the broader economy. During the distribution stage, investors may become more cautious and less optimistic about the future prospects of the companies whose stocks they are selling, leading to further price declines.

   The distribution stage can be a good time for investors to buy undervalued stocks, as prices are likely to be low. However, it's essential to be cautious during this phase, as declining stock prices can sometimes signify broader economic problems.

4. Markdown Stage :

The final stage of the stock market cycle, the markdown stage, is *not a good time for most investors*. The traders who bought stocks during the distribution phase would try to sell their positions as they see losses. However, some buyers are present to meet the sale of these shares. This lack of demand drives the prices of stocks to further lower levels & may finally reach a particular level where the demand is high enough.

The chart below (Fig.5.2) is another example where you can clearly see the four stages mentioned earlier.

(Fig. 5.2)

It's worth noting that these stages are not always clearly defined, and the duration and intensity of each stage may vary. Some market cycles may not go through the trough or markdown stage at all, and instead go straight from contraction to recovery.

CHAPTER 6
Technical Indicators

Technical Analysis is studied with the help of various indicators, which are essential technical tools that help us to know the momentum, trend, volatility and range of the market or a stock.

There are over 100's of technical indicators in the market that serve different purposes. However, in this book, I will focus on the most popular ones & the ones which the most profitable traders widely use.

Here are a few essential things to remember before we begin:

- Using multiple indicators simultaneously can be confusing and affect your decision's accuracy. So always apply just a few selected indicators properly to initiate a clear position or trade.
- There is no single indicator that suits all market conditions.
- Indicators are beneficial for predicting future trends, alerting before the reversal, and confirming the trend. Some indicators help to know the momentum, while some help to see the trend. Some indicators can show us the trend's strength, while others can also help us get trend reversal signals.

Knowing how to use technical indicators is very important to achieving success in technical analysis. We will learn about some of these technical indicators in the upcoming section.

Technical indicators, broadly, are of two types - Lagging and Leading. Both leading and lagging indicators perform different functions.

Lagging Indicators :

Lagging indicators, also called trend-following indicators, are more suitable in the trending market but ineffective in the sideways market.
Their main benefit is that it enables the trader to catch a move and remain in a move.
But their drawback is that they give late signals.
Some of the most widely used lagging indicators are :

1.1 Moving Averages
1.2 MACD indicator

1.1 Moving Averages

There is always going to be a lot of volatility or noise around in the market. Those who see & follow charts can relate to this better. A moving average cuts out this noise or random market fluctuations and gives the average price value over a given duration.

So a 10-day moving average (DMA) or 10 DMA means the average value of the closing prices from Day 1 to Day 10. Similarly, a 200 DMA will take the average of the closing price of the past 200 days. Don't worry; you do not have to calculate the moving average manually. Instead, you can easily plot the moving averages below the price using any charting software.

There are two types of Moving Averages :

Simple Moving Average (SMA) and Exponential Moving Average (EMA)

A Simple Moving Average, or SMA, is less sensitive than the Exponential Moving average or EMA. That's why SMA's react slower to market changes than EMA's.

This is the precise reason why most traders prefer using EMA's only.

EMA's will stay closer or farther from the price depending on the time period. This is because the shorter period moving average is based on fewer data points & a long period moving average has more data points which may be placed farther from each other.

Let us understand EMA on an actual chart. Check out chart 31.

You can see that the 5 EMA (yellow line) stays closer to the price when compared to a 20 EMA (pink line) signal.

The 5 EMA line acts as a dynamic support to the price action. However, note that it is still a lagging indicator only & will continue to follow the price.

There is a clear uptrend in the chart & the same can be seen from the upward slope of both the EMA's.

(Chart 31)

in most cases, the price will stay above the moving average if it is an uptrend. Therefore, a trader can have a bullish bias for such stocks & can enter accordingly when the price is closer to the moving average.

On the contrary, if a stock is falling, the moving average line will slope downwards & confirm the downtrend. A trader can then have a bearish bias for the particular stock & may enter a short position.

Check out chart 32 to know how EMA's look in a downtrend :

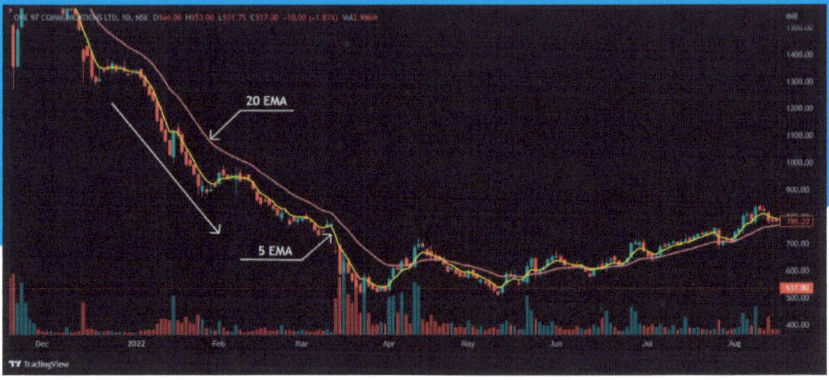

(Chart 32)

How to Buy/Sell a Stock using EMA alone?

Now that you have understood how EMA works ,have a look at chart 33.

(Chart 33)

As seen in chart 33 - Finolex Cables (Daily Timeframe), we have plotted only 2 EMA's -50 EMA & 100 EMA.

You can see that when the 50 EMA has a negative crossover with the 100 EMA line, it is referred to as a Dead Cross & is a Sell Signal, which means if you are holding a Long position in this stock, you must exit at the Dead cross. You may also build a new short position in the stock at this time.

When there is a positive crossover between 50 EMA & 100 EMA, it is referred to as the *Golden Cross* & one can enter a new long position at this point.

So this is how only EMA's can be used for Entry & Exits.

1.2 MACD indicator :

The MACD (Moving Average Convergence Divergence) is a technical indicator used in stock and commodity trading to identify changes in the momentum and trend of a market.

It is calculated using the difference between a short-term moving average (12-day EMA) and a long-term moving average (26-day EMA) of a security's price. A 9-day EMA of the MACD line, called the "signal line," is plotted along with the MACD to generate trading signals. Refer chart no. 34.

MACD has no limit on upside or downside, but it has a zero mean. MACD tends to oscillate around this zero mean as the moving averages converge, intersect and diverge.

Convergence is said to occur when the moving averages move towards each other. Similarly, Divergence happens when the moving averages move away from each other. The MACD histogram is below 0 when the shorter moving average is below the longer moving average and above 0 when the 12-period moving average is above the 26-period moving average. The MACD is often used to generate buy and sell signals based on the cross of the MACD line and the signal line,

Chart 34 shows how the MACD indicator looks when plotted.

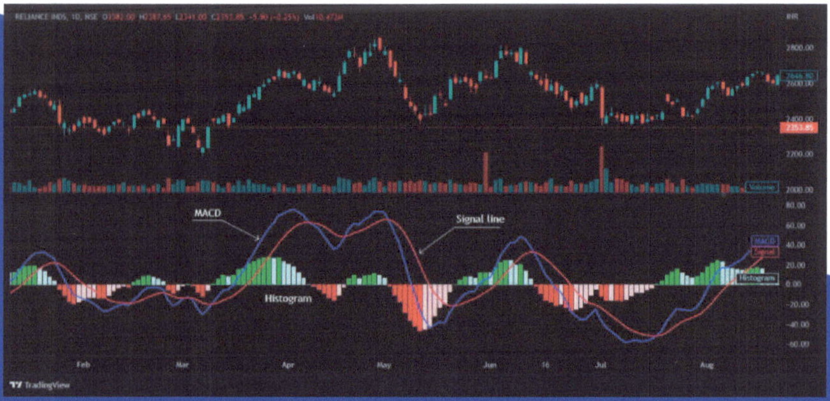

(Chart 34)

The MACD can also be used as an oscillator. The stock market always returns to the mean, and the fast-moving average always returns to the slower one. The more significant the difference between the moving averages (the higher the MACD histogram is), the more bearish the market is, and the greater the possibility of a price correction that will bring MACD back to 0.

Chart 35 shows the MACD at extreme highs.

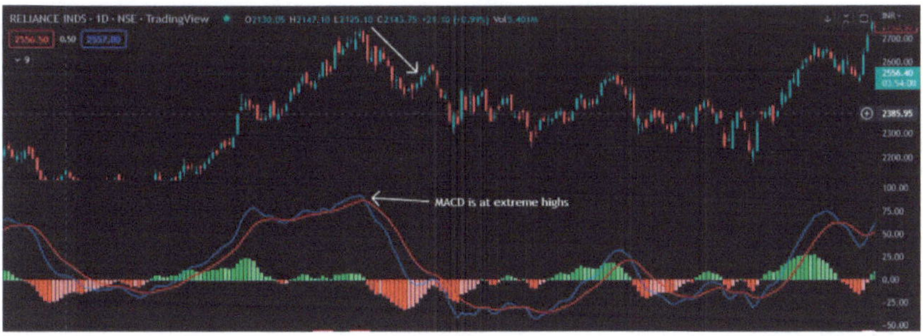

(Chart 35)

The lower the MACD, the higher the probability of the stock making a bullish reversal from the lowest point.

Check out chart 36.It shows MACD at extreme lows.

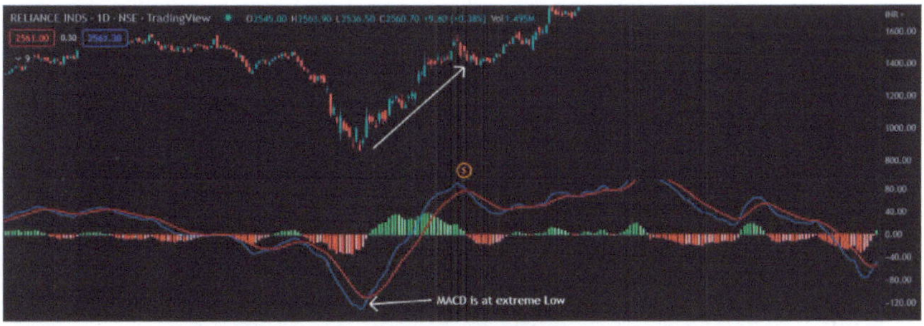

(Chart 36)

So this is how you can analyze the stock movement using the MACD indicator.

Though MACD is a Lagging indicator, with the concept of divergence, it can also be used as a Leading indicator.

Leading Indicators :

Leading indicators in technical analysis are data points used to predict future price changes. The main benefit of these indicators is getting signals of early entry and exit. Leading technical indicators examine the data received from past price movements and try to pre-empt or predict future price movements. They enable traders to anticipate future price movements.

Indicators like MACD and RSI (Relative Strength Index) can be used as Leading indicators by knowing certain concepts. Let's understand how.

Firstly, let's understand the RSI indicator.

2.1 Relative Strength Index (RSI) Indicator :

A leading momentum indicator, RSI helps in identifying a trend reversal. It fluctuates between 0 and 100. Based on the latest indicator reading, market prediction is made.

Here is how the RSI indicator will look once plotted on the chart (chart 37), along with the price.

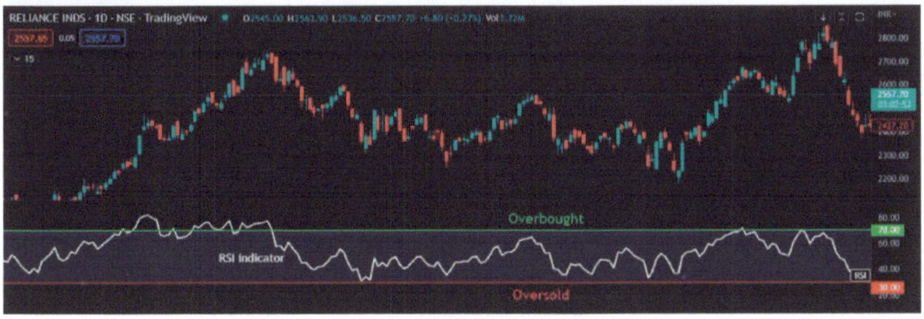

(Chart 37)

Chart 38 shows how RSI can be used as a Leading indicator using Divergence :

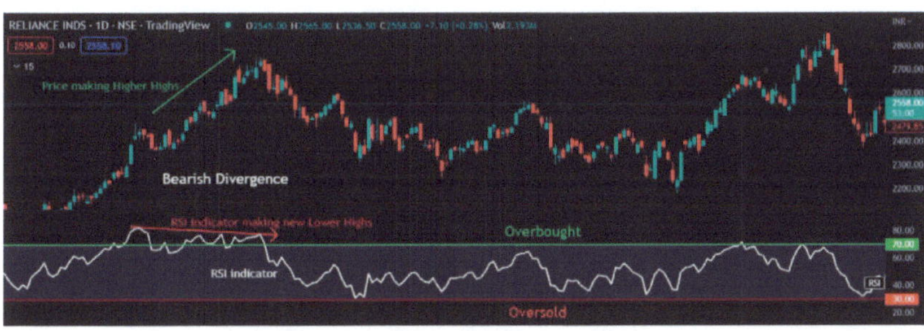

(Chart 38)

RSI is a momentum oscillator fluctuating between 0 to 100 levels.

A value between 0 and 30 is regarded to be oversold. So, the trader should look at buying opportunities.

A value between 70 and 100 is regarded to be overbought. So, a trader should look at selling opportunities.

If the RSI value is constant in a section for a lengthy period, it indicates excess momentum. Hence, rather than taking on a reversed position, one can consider initiating a trade in the same direction.

Bearish divergence - (as seen in chart 38) is formed when the price makes new Higher Highs & the RSI indicator makes new Lower Highs simultaneously. A trader is expected to exit his Long position or enter a fresh Short Position once a Bearish divergence is seen.

Similarly, **a Bullish divergence** (as seen in chart 39) is formed when the price makes Lower Lows & corresponding RSI indicator makes Higher Lows. Therefore, a trader is expected to exit his Short position or enter a fresh Long Position once a Bullish divergence is seen.

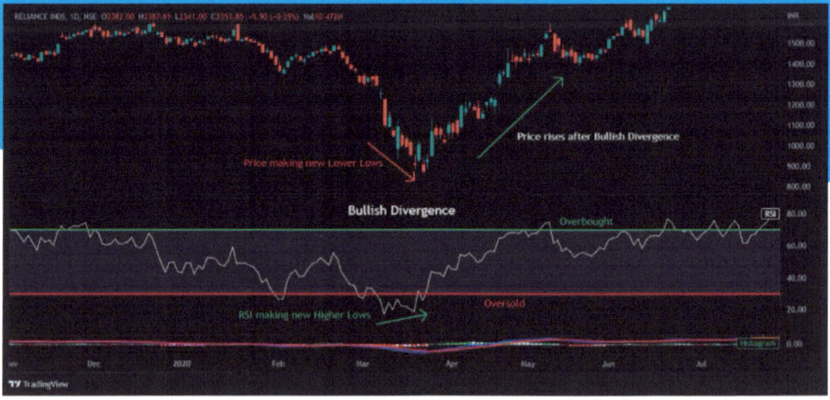

(Chart 39)

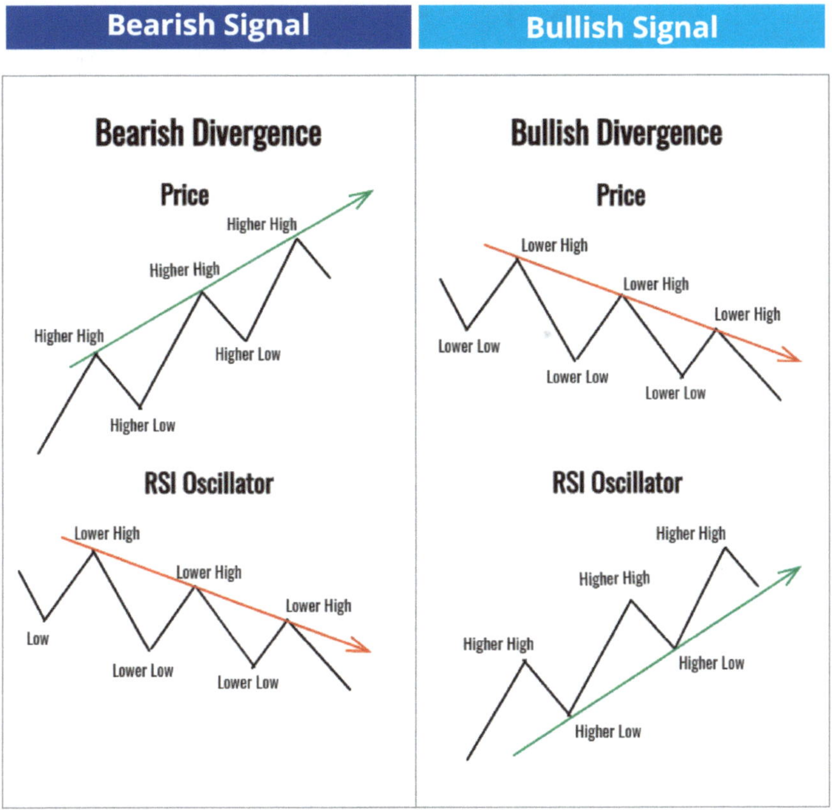

(Fig. 6.1)

2.2 Pivot Points :

Pivot points are levels of support and resistance calculated using the high, low, and close prices of a stock or index over a specified time frame. They are widely used in technical analysis as potential levels of support and resistance.

Chart 40, a 5 min timeframe of the Nifty 50 index, shows how the Pivot Points would look on charts.

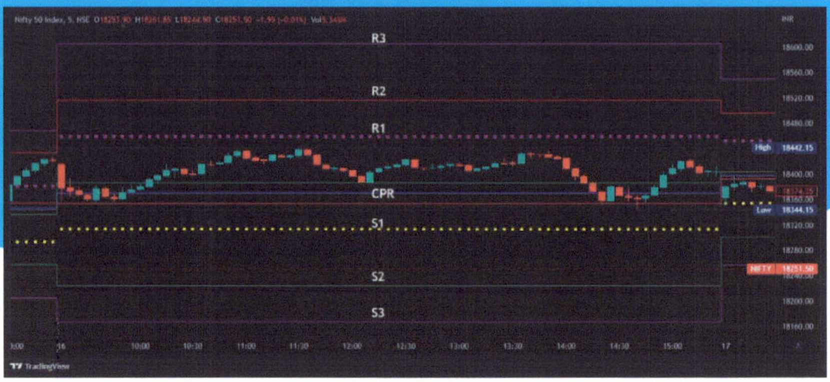

(Chart 40)

The Central Pivot Range (CPR), also known as the pivot range, is the range between the first support (S1 - denoted by a yellow dotted line in chart 40) and the first resistance (R1 - denoted by a purple dotted line in chart 40) in a pivot point calculation. The pivot range is considered to be the most important aspect of the pivot point indicator, as it is used to identify potential levels of support and resistance for the security's price movement.

CPP stands for Central Pivot Point which lies at the center of CPR & is denoted by a blue line as seen in chart 40.

The most commonly used pivot point formula is the five-point pivot point calculation, which involves calculating the following values:

CPP = (High + Low + Close) / 3

R1 = 1st Resistance

R1 = (2*CPP) - Low

R2 = 2nd Resistance
R2 = CPP + (High - Low)

R3 = 3rd Resistance
R3 = R1 + (High - Low)

S1 = 1st Support
S1 = (2*CPP) - High

S2 = 2nd Support
S2 = CPP - (High - Low)

S3 = 3rd Support
S3 = S1 - (High - Low)

Note that 'High' & 'Low' used in the formula are the previous day's high & low data points.

So you can see that all the pivot points on the chart are calculated using the previous day's price action data. You do not need to calculate any of this manually, as the CPR indicator is readily available on any charting platform.

Suppose you plot indicators like MACD, RSI, EMA etc on a chart, you will observe that in every timeframe, they give different signals & hence you may find it confusing at times.

But ***pivots are fixed on the chart irrespective of timeframe*** (as they are calculated using the previous day's price action data). They are the same in any timeframe - 3 minutes, 5 minutes, 15 minutes or 1-hour chart or 4-hour chart.

Pivot levels are nothing but supports and resistances & their roles reverse when price action breaks any level.

Since CPR can be calculated before market opening, it helps traders in multiple ways, from position sizing to deciding stop loss levels upfront.

CPR can also be helpful in the analysis of trends over multiple days.

(Chart 41)

- An uptrend will always have a Rising CPR.
- The CPR will act as a support in an Uptrend.
- Once the CPR breaks, one can exit the Long position. The same can be seen in the above image.
- Closing the above day's CPR tells you to have a bullish bias for the following day.

- Lastly, avoid buying a stock when its price is far from the CPR point. Buy only when it is near or close to the CPR.

Check out chart 42 showing a downtrend.

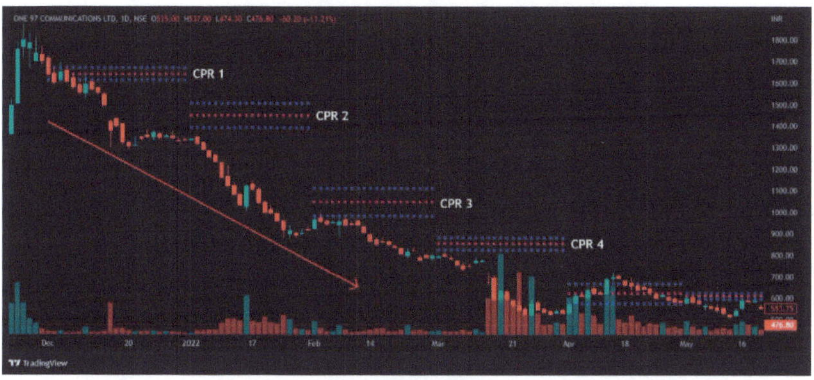

(Chart 42)

- A downtrend will always have a falling CPR
- The CPR will act as a resistance and restrict prices from moving to higher levels.
- Price closing below the CPR tells you to have a bearish bias for the next day.
- Wider CPR = Sideways day (Most of the time, NOT Always)
- Narrow CPR = Trending Day (Most of the time, NOT Always)

Traders and investors use CPR & pivot points as potential levels of support and resistance, and watch for price to either break through these levels or find support or resistance at them.

Takeaways:

- Technical indicators are mathematical calculations based on the price and/or volume of a security. They are used to help traders make informed decisions by providing information on trends & momentum.
- Trend indicators - provide information on the direction of a security's price. Examples include moving averages and trend lines.
- Momentum indicators - measure the strength of a security's price action. Examples include Relative Strength Index (RSI) and Moving Average Convergence Divergence (MACD).
- It is important to use multiple technical indicators in conjunction to validate trade signals and reduce the risk of false signals.
- Technical indicators are subject to interpretation and may produce false signals, therefore it is important to use them in a strategic and systematic manner as part of a comprehensive trading plan.

CHAPTER 7
Key Price Action Patterns

In the exciting and complex world of technical analysis, one realm stands apart for its inherent visual appeal and analytical richness—Price Action Chart Patterns. As a Certified Technical Analyst, my main aim in this chapter is to introduce you to these fascinating patterns and demonstrate how useful they are for navigating the rough waters of stock market trading.

Chart patterns form the bedrock of technical analysis and provide critical insights into the never-ending narrative of supply and demand that drives all markets. These patterns distil millions of trading decisions into recognizable, predictive shapes on price charts. They reflect the psychology of market participants and offer predictions about future price movements.

This chapter will overview the most significant and commonly observed chart patterns. These include but are not limited to, Reversal Patterns like Head and Shoulders, Double Tops and Bottoms, Continuation Patterns like Flags, Pennants, and Triangles, and Bilateral Patterns like Rectangles and Symmetrical Triangles, which can break out in either way.
For each pattern, we will delve into its construction and the

underlying psychology, the rules for its confirmation, and its potential implications for future price movement. I have done my best to give you understandable examples from the real world, along with helpful advice on applying these patterns to make entry, exit, and risk management decisions.

Remember, while chart patterns have proven their worth over time, they should not be used in isolation. Additional techniques for technical analysis, like trend lines, moving averages, and momentum indicators, can provide essential context and increase the odds of success when combined with price action chart patterns.

This chapter aims to make you comfortable spotting and interpreting these patterns in live markets and eventually using them to formulate successful trading strategies.
Remember that, as in all trading and investment, **there are no guarantees—only probabilities.** Understanding and applying these chart patterns will not lead to sure success but will certainly tilt the odds in your favour. This, in essence, is the goal of every successful trader.

Now, let's embark on this fascinating journey through the visual language of markets!
Welcome to the world of Key Price Action Chart Patterns!

1. **Head & Shoulders Pattern:**

   The Head and Shoulders pattern (Fig 7.1) is a widely recognized chart pattern in technical analysis. It typically signals a potential trend reversal from an uptrend to a downtrend. The pattern gets its name from its visual similarity to a head with two shoulders.

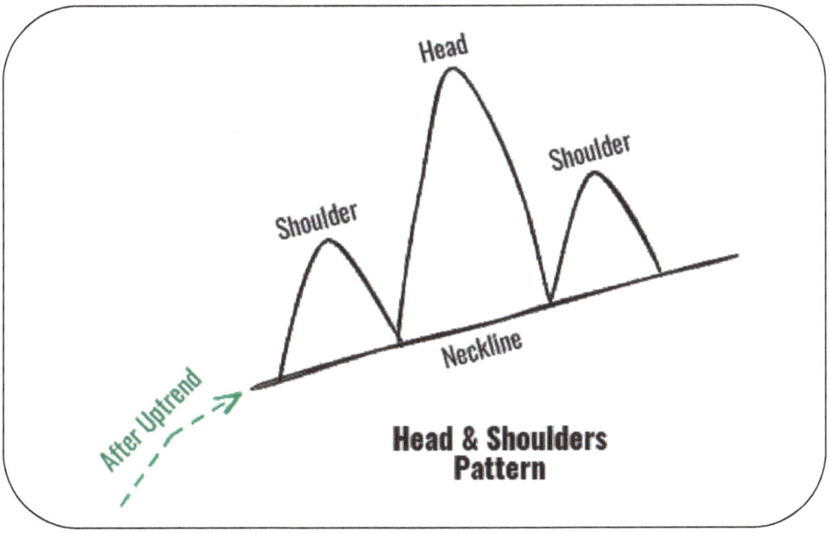

(Fig. 7.1)

Three successive peaks form this pattern. The first and third peaks, called 'Shoulders', are roughly equal in height, while the second peak, the 'Head', is the highest. The line connecting the lows after the first and second peaks is called the 'Neckline'. **Note that the neckline can be perfectly horizontal or even inclined, as shown in the above image.**

Head & Shoulders Pattern Identification Checklist (Fig 7.2):

- **Left Shoulder:** The stock is in an uptrend, with the price reaching a new high, followed by a decline to a low.
- **Head:** A rally then ensues, creating a higher high, followed by a decline that stops near the same low area as the first decline, making the neckline.
- **Right Shoulder:** The stock attempts to rally once more, but this rally fails before it reaches the height of the head, indicating a possible loss of momentum. The right shoulder is thus formed. The subsequent decline again touches the neckline.

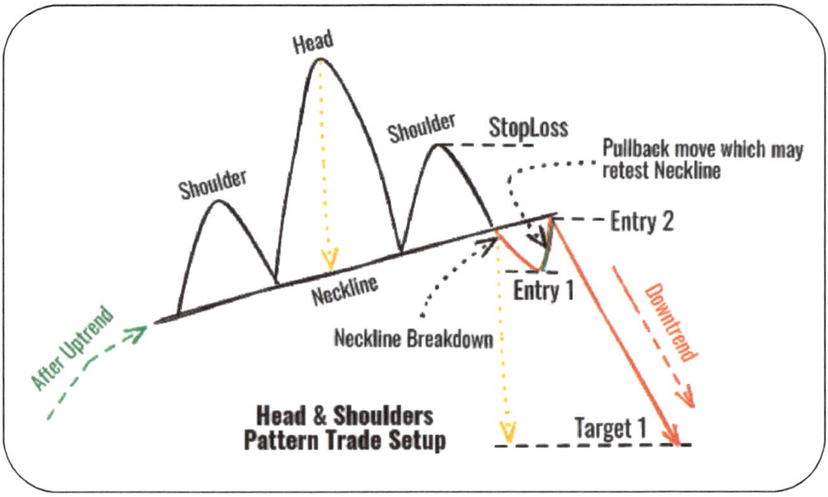

(Fig. 7.2)

Head & Shoulders Pattern Trade Setup (Fig 7.2)

- **Entry**

  An entry point is typically triggered when the price closes below the neckline after forming the right shoulder. This is the confirmation of the pattern. It is advised to wait for this confirmation before initiating a short position rather than predicting the completion of the pattern prematurely. Most of the time (not always), there might be a pullback which retests the neckline & this becomes your Entry 2.

- **Exit**

  One can estimate the price target or the exit point by measuring the distance from the neckline to the top of the head, as shown in yellow. This distance is then subtracted from the point where the price breaks through the neckline.

- **Stop Loss**

  A stop loss is typically placed just above the right shoulder. This way, the loss is limited if the pattern fails and the price reverses upward.

While the Head & Shoulders pattern is a powerful tool, it's crucial to remember that no pattern works 100% of the time. Therefore, it's essential to use other technical indicators or tools, such as volume or moving averages, to confirm the pattern and mitigate risk.

Case Study 43 : Nifty50 -1 hr Timeframe- 3rd Nov 2022 to 15 Dec 2022 (Chart 43)

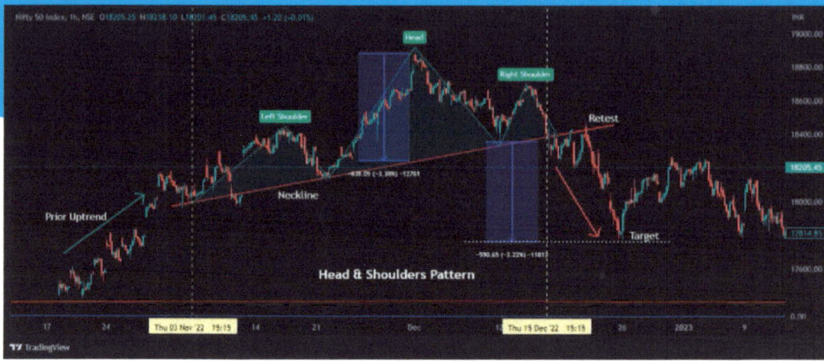

(Chart 43)

2. **Inverted Head and Shoulders (Inverted H&S):**
   This pattern (Fig 7.3) is typically formed at the bottom of a downward trend. It signals a potential bullish reversal (a transition from a downtrend to an uptrend).

Inverted Head & Shoulders Pattern Identification Checklist (Fig 7.3):

- ✓ Three troughs make up the pattern, which is essentially an upside-down H&S.
- ✓ The centre trough, or Head, is the deepest, while the two outer troughs, or Shoulders, are shallower and about equal.
- ✓ The line connecting the high points of the troughs is the "neckline." A break above the neckline confirms the pattern.

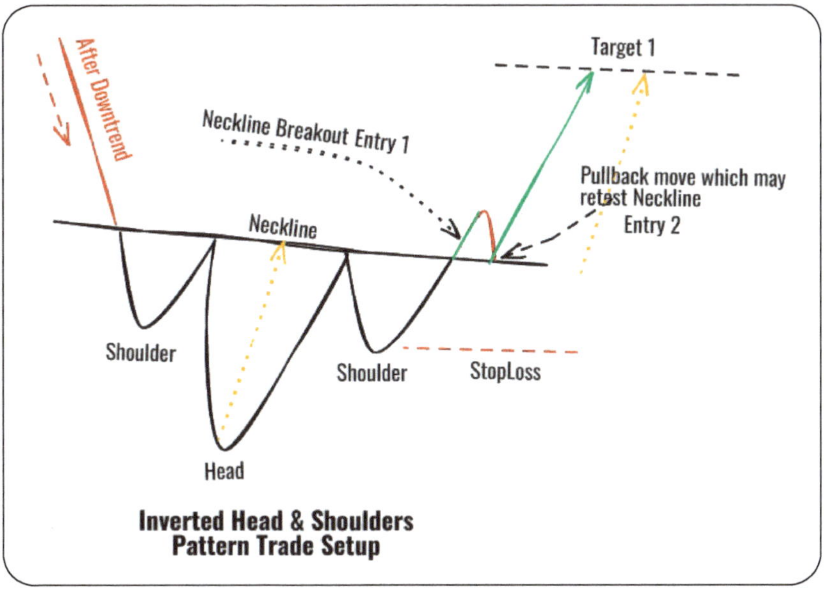

(Fig. 7.3)

Inverted Head & Shoulders Pattern Trade Setup (Fig 7.3)

Entry

You should consider entering a long position (buy) when the price breaks above the neckline (Entry 1) after the formation of the right shoulder. This breakout is your signal that the downtrend may be reversing. An alternative entry may be taken (Entry 2) at the pullback if and when it happens. Ideally, the breakout should occur with an increase in volume, which adds confirmation to the bullish reversal.

- **Exit**

  The exit point, or the target price, can be estimated by calculating the distance from the head to the neckline. You would then extend this distance upward from the breakout point at the neckline. This gives you a rough idea of how far the price might rise following the breakout.

- **Stop Loss**

  After you enter a trade, setting a stop-loss order to manage your risk is crucial. A common place to set a stop-loss is just below the right shoulder. This is because if the price falls back to this level, it might suggest that the bullish reversal was false.

Keep an eye on the price as it moves towards your target. You can move your stop-loss up to lock in profits or exit the trade early if the price action suggests that the trend is reversing again.

Case Study 44 : Nifty50 index-Daily Timeframe - 22nd Feb 2023 to 28th April 2023 (Chart 44)

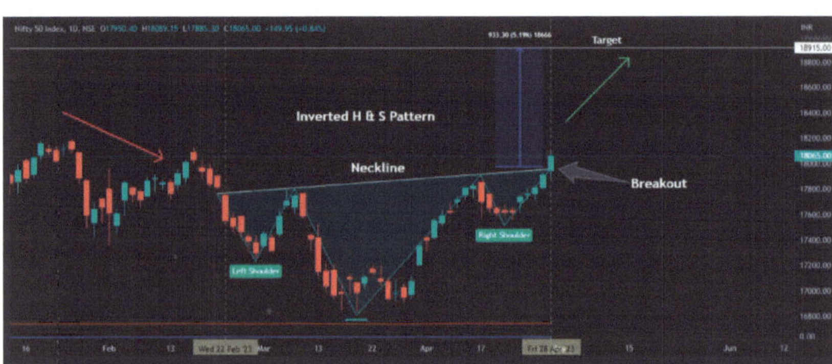

(Chart 44)

Case Study 45 : Nifty50 index-Daily Timeframe - 3rd Nov 2022 to 15 Dec 2022 & 22nd Feb 2023 to 28th April 2023 (Chart 45)

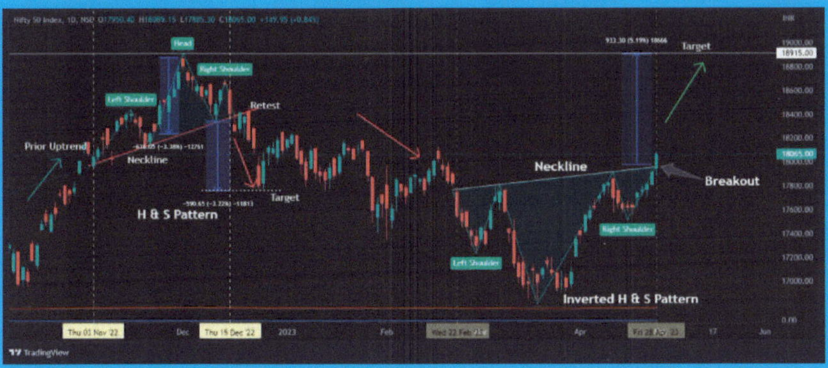

(Chart 45)

Chart 45 shows both the H&S pattern & Inverted H&S Pattern formation on the Nifty50 index. When writing this book, the neckline of the Inverted H&S pattern is broken & the target comes out to be 18915. It will be interesting to see if this target is met or not in future.

For better understanding, please take a moment to compare Chart 45 with the current Nifty50 chart and analyze them.

3. Double Tops or "M" Top

The Double Tops chart pattern (Fig.7.4) is popular among technical analysts and traders, signalling a potential reversal in an upward trend. It gets its name from the 'M' shape it forms on the chart, with two distinct peaks or 'tops' at roughly the same price level.

Double Tops or "M" Top Pattern Identification checklist (Fig 7.4):

- **First Top:** When the price increases to a new high during an uptrend, producing the first top, the pattern is said to have begun. A retracement or a price decline follows this.
- **Second Top:** After the retracement, the price then rallies back to the previous high, forming the second top, which is approximately at the same level as the first. However, the price fails to break above this level, indicating potential exhaustion in the buying pressure.
- **Neckline:** The lows reached after the formation of each top can be connected to form the 'neckline'.

Double Tops or "M" Top Pattern Trade Setup (Fig 7.4):

- **Entry**

  The confirmation of the Double Top pattern, and thus the signal to enter a trade, typically occurs when the price closes below the neckline after forming the second top. Traders often initiate a short position at this point.
- **Exit**

  The distance between the neckline and the pattern's top is vertically measured, and this measurement is then subtracted from the neckline to determine the price target or the exit point.
- **Stop Loss**

  A stop loss order can be placed slightly above the high of the second top. This way, the loss can be minimized if the price doesn't follow through with the anticipated downward move and reverses upwards.

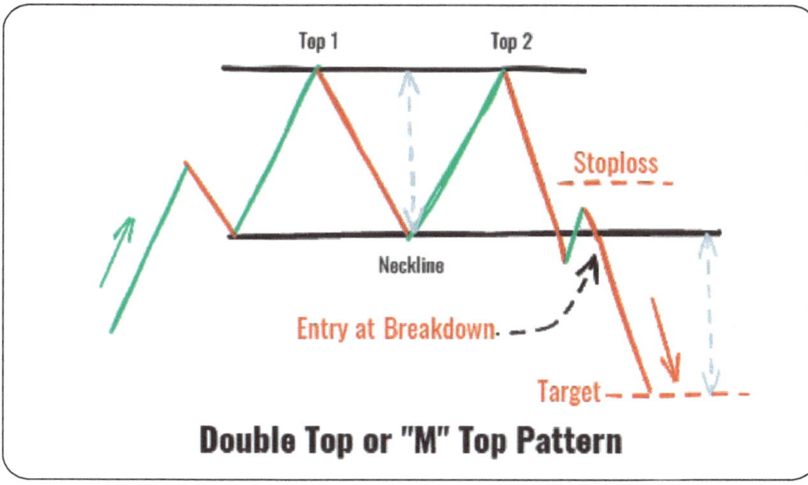

(Fig. 7.4)

It's important to note that while the Double Top pattern can be a valuable tool in predicting potential market reversals, no single chart pattern is infallible. Therefore, it is essential to use additional technical indicators or chart patterns to confirm signals and manage risk.

Case Study 46: Crude oil Futures - 2hr Timeframe - 22nd December 2022 to 4th January 2023 (Chart 46)

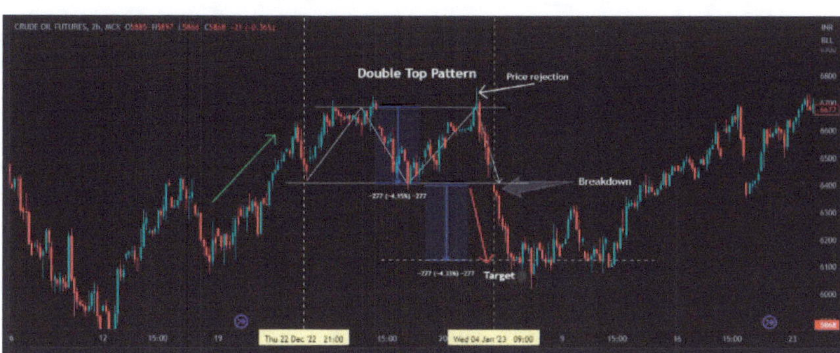

(Chart 46)

4. **Double Bottom :**

The Double Bottom chart pattern (Fig 7.5) is a favourite among technical traders and analysts. It signals a potential bullish reversal, typically appearing at the end of a downtrend. The pattern is named for its "W" shape, with two distinct troughs or 'bottoms' at roughly the same price level.

Double Bottom Pattern Identification checklist (Fig 7.5) :

- **First Bottom:** Price lowers to a new low, forming the first bottom and a rally, and the pattern starts during a downtrend.
- **Second Bottom:** After the rally, the price then falls back to the previous low, forming the second bottom, which is approximately at the same level as the first. However, the price fails to break below this level, indicating potential exhaustion in the selling pressure.
- **Neckline:** The highs reached after the formation of each bottom can be connected to form the 'neckline'.

  Double Bottom Pattern Trade Setup (Fig 7.5):

- **Entry**

  The Double Bottom pattern is typically confirmed when the price closes above the neckline after forming the second bottom. This is often considered an ideal entry point to initiate a long position.

Exit

The price objective or exit point may be decided by measuring the distance from the neckline to the bottom of the pattern vertically and adding this measurement to the neckline.

Stop Loss

A stop loss order is usually placed slightly below the low of the second bottom. This way, the loss can be minimized if the price doesn't confirm the pattern and reverses downwards.

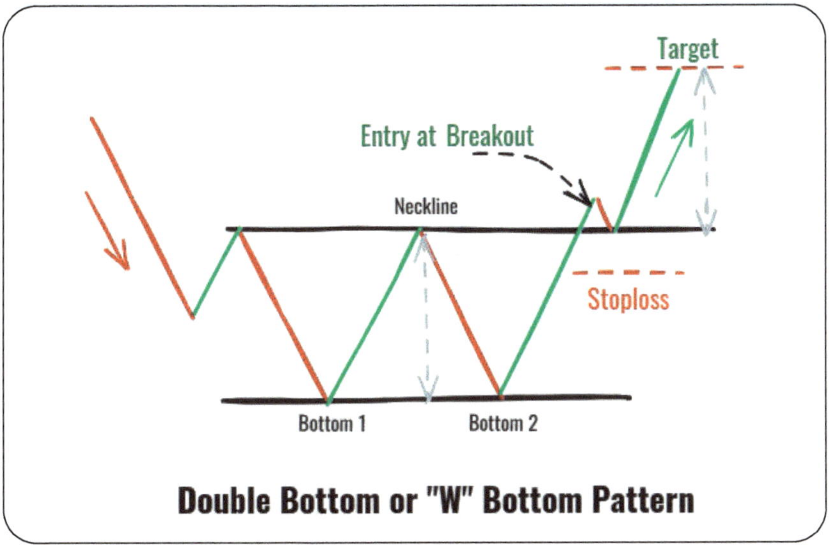

(Fig. 7.5)

It's important to remember that while the Double Bottom pattern can be a potent tool in predicting potential market reversals, no single chart pattern is foolproof. As such, it's crucial to use additional technical indicators or chart patterns to confirm signals and manage risk.

Case Study 47: Wipro Ltd-Daily Timeframe -17th March 2023 to 27th April 2023 (Chart 47)

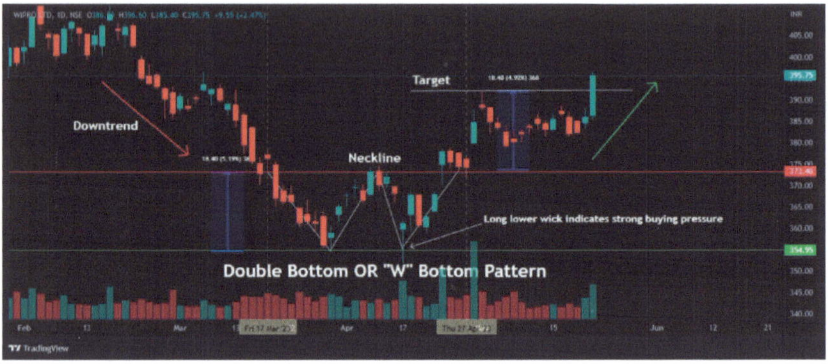

(Chart 47)

5. **Continuation Pattern:**

   Continuation patterns are powerful tools in technical analysis, indicating that an existing trend is likely to continue after a brief pause. They provide insights into potential trade opportunities, giving traders an idea of where prices might be headed.

   Two of the most popular continuation patterns are Flags and Pennants. These patterns are commonly seen after a big, quick move in the price of a stock, followed by a shorter period of consolidation before the original trend resumes.

A. Flags

Continuation patterns, such as the Flag pattern, are essential tools in technical analysis. Usually, they happen in the middle of a trend and signal a pause in the price movement before the original trend resumes. Here, we will discuss the Flag & Pole pattern, which looks like a small rectangle or a parallelogram sloping against the prevailing trend and a pole.

Flag & Pole Pattern Identification Checklist (Fig 7.6):

- The Flag & Pole pattern begins with a strong, near-vertical price movement, known as the Pole, which forms the main upward or downward trend.
- Following the Pole, the price consolidates and moves in a tight range against the trend, forming the Flag. This typically occurs on lower volume.

Depending on the initial trend direction, the Flag pattern may be bullish or bearish. A Bullish Flag follows an uptrend and indicates a potential continuation of the uptrend after the pattern completes. In contrast, a Bearish Flag follows a downtrend and suggests a possible continuation of the downtrend.

Flag & Pole Pattern Trade Setup (Fig 7.6):

- **Entry**

  An entry signal is typically generated when the price breaks out of the flag in the direction of the prevailing trend. For a Bullish Flag, this would be a breakout above the upper boundary of the flag. For a Bearish Flag, it would be a breakout below the lower boundary of the flag.

Exit

The price target or exit point is calculated by measuring the length of the flagpole and projecting this distance from the breakout point. For example, if a Bullish Flag's pole is 10 points tall, and the breakout occurs at 50, the target price would be 60 (50 + 10).

Stop Loss

A stop-loss order is generally placed outside the flag's boundary opposite the breakout. So, for a Bullish Flag, a stop loss could be placed slightly below the lower boundary of the flag.

It's crucial to remember that while the Flag pattern can be an effective tool in predicting trend continuation, no single chart pattern is infallible. Therefore, it is advisable to use additional technical indicators or chart patterns to confirm signals and manage risk.

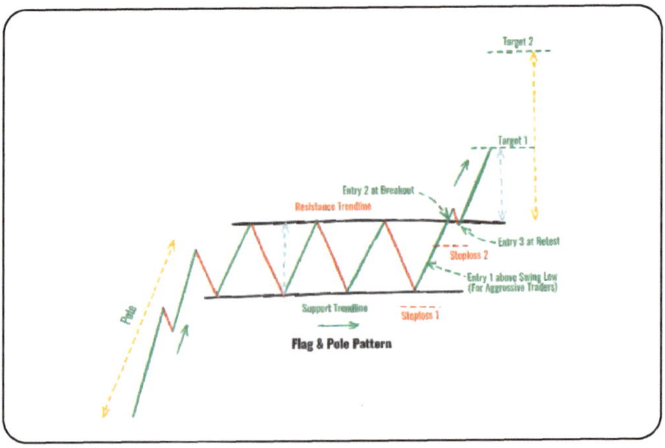

(Fig. 7.6)

Case Study 48: CG Power Ltd.- Daily Timeframe - 3rd January 2022 to 21st July 2022 (Chart 48)

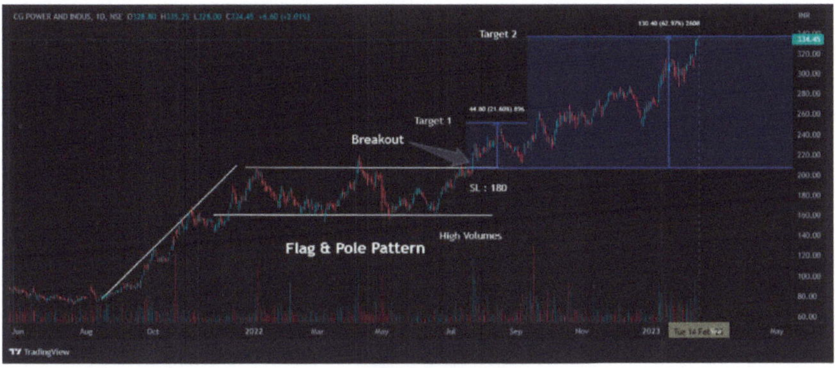

(Chart 48)

B. Pennants:

Pennant patterns are commonly used in technical analysis as a reliable indicator of trend continuation. The pattern's name refers to how it resembles a pennant flag flying on a pole.

Like Flags, Pennants signal a pause or consolidation in the middle of a trend before the original trend resumes.

Unlike Flags, however, Pennants are small symmetrical triangles.

Pennant Pattern Identification Checklist (Fig 7.7 & Fig 7.8):

- The Pennant pattern begins with a sharp, near-vertical price movement, known as the flagpole, forming the main trend, either upward or downward.
- Following the pole, the price consolidates and moves in a tightening range, forming the 'Pennant'. This is usually characterized by converging trend lines and occurs on lower volume.
- Like Flag patterns, Pennants can be bullish or bearish, depending on the initial trend direction. A Bullish Pennant (Fig 7.7) follows an uptrend and indicates a potential continuation of the uptrend after the pattern completes. In contrast, a Bearish Pennant (Fig 7.8) follows a downtrend and signals a potential continuation of the downtrend.

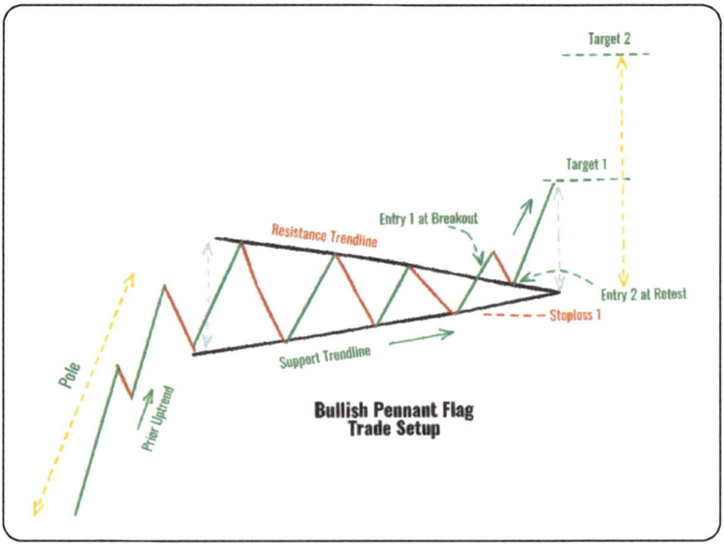

(Fig. 7.7)

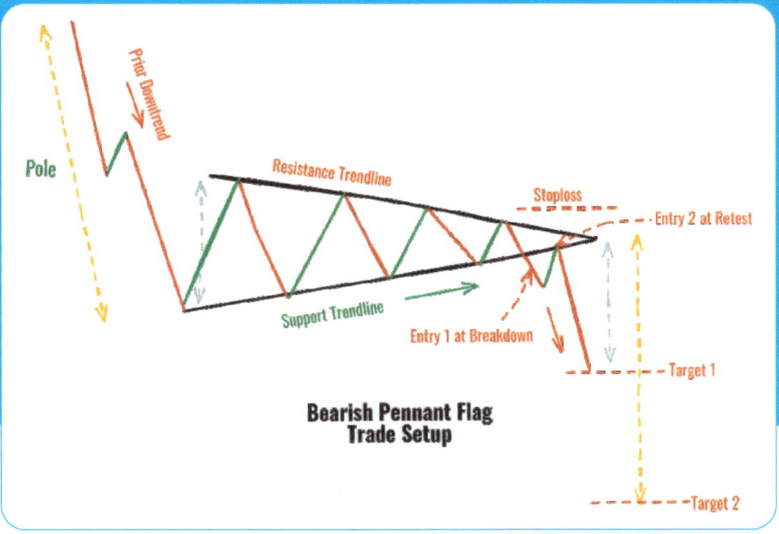

(Fig. 7.8)

Pennant Pattern Trade Setup (Fig 7.7 & Fig.7.8):

- **Entry**

  The price breaking out of the pennant in the direction of the prevailing trend is typically the best entry point. For a Bullish Pennant, this would be a breakout above the upper trend line of the pennant. A breakout below the bottom trend line of the pennant would indicate a Bearish Pennant.

- **Exit**

  The first price target or exit point is the width of the pennant. The second target is calculated by measuring the length of the flagpole and projecting this distance from the breakout point. For example, if a Bullish Pennant's pole is 10 points tall, and the breakout occurs at 50/-, the target price would be 60/- (50 + 10).

Stop Loss

A stop-loss order is generally placed just outside the pennant's boundary opposite the breakout. So, for a Bullish Pennant, a stop loss could be placed slightly below the lower trend line of the pennant.

Case Study 49: Silver Futures.- Daily Timeframe - 13th May 2020 to 29th June 2020 (Chart 49).

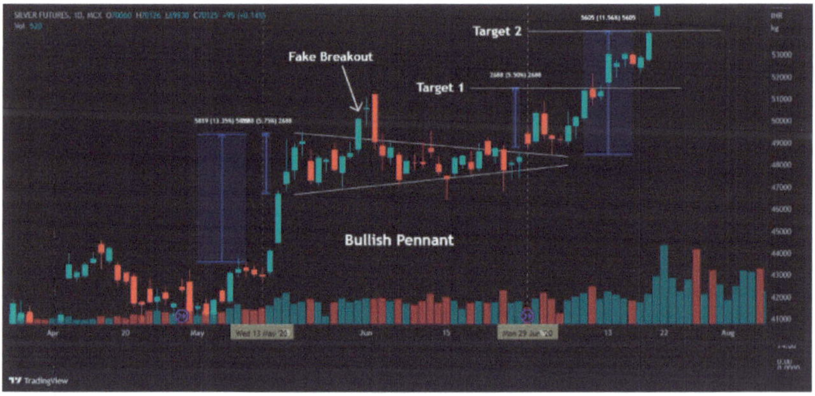

(Chart 49)

6. Triangles Pattern :

Triangle patterns are classic chart formations used in technical analysis to predict breakout directions and potentially significant price moves. There are three main types of triangles: Ascending, Descending, and Symmetrical.

A. Ascending Triangle :

An Ascending Triangle is typically considered a bullish pattern and is usually found in an uptrend.

Ascending Triangle Identification (Fig 7.9): This pattern forms when there's a resistance level and a trendline drawn along higher lows.

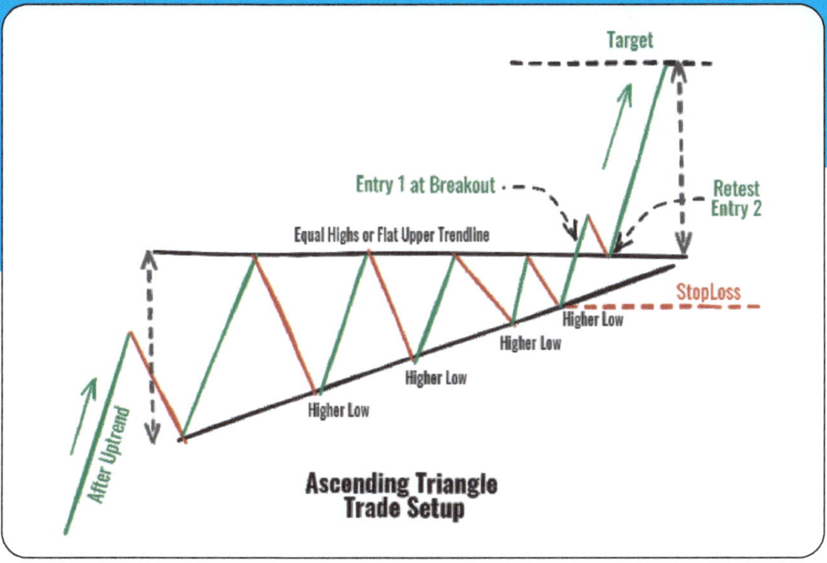

(Fig. 7.9)

Ascending Triangle Pattern Trade Setup (Fig 7.9):

- **Entry:** The Buy signal occurs when the price breaks out above the resistance level.
- **Exit:** The price target is calculated by adding the vertical height of the triangle to the breakout price. One can continue to stay in the trade with a Trailing Stoploss to capture the maximum move.
- **Stop Loss:** A stop loss can be placed just below the upward-sloping trendline or the most recent low within the triangle.

Case Study 50 : Hari Om Pipe Industries - Daily Timeframe - 25th August 2022 to 25th November 2022 (Chart 50)

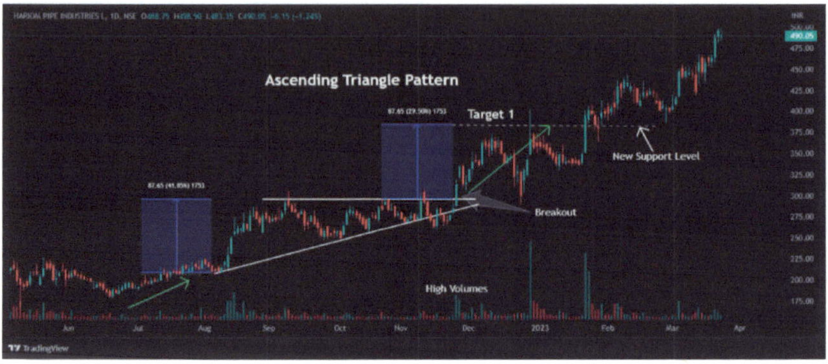

(Chart 50)

B. Descending Triangle

In contrast to the symmetrical triangle pattern, a descending triangle has a definite bearish bias before the actual break. A Descending Triangle is typically considered a bearish pattern usually found in a downtrend.

Descending Triangle Identification (Fig 7.10) : This pattern forms when there's a support level and a trendline drawn along lower highs

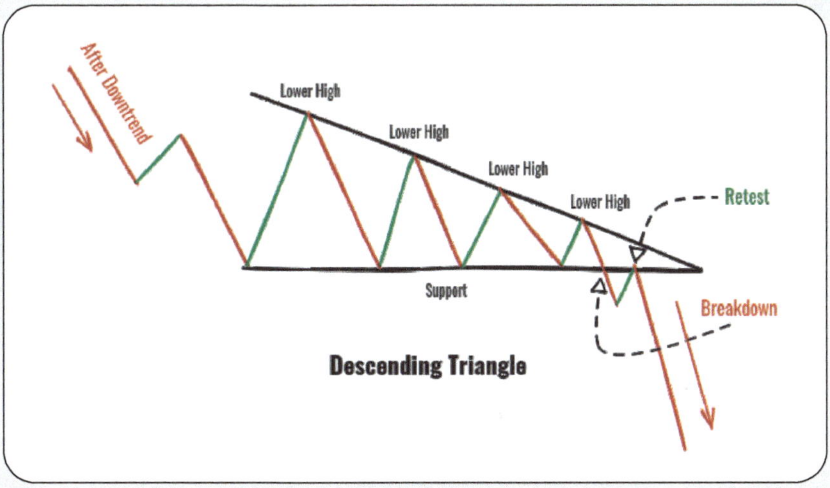

(Fig 7.10)

Descending Triangle Pattern Trade Setup (Fig.7.10)

- **Entry:** The sell signal occurs when the price breaks down below the support level.
- **Exit:** The price target is calculated by subtracting the vertical height of the triangle from the breakdown price.
- **Stop Loss:** A stop loss can be placed just above the downward-sloping trendline or the most recent high within the triangle.

Case Study 51: Crude Oil Futures- Daily Timeframe- 22nd November 2022 to 13th March 2023 (Chart 51)

(Chart 51)

C. Symmetrical Triangle

Symmetrical Triangles can be a continuation or reversal pattern depending on the context and can break out in either direction.

Symmetrical Triangle Identification (Fig 7.11 to Fig.7.14): This pattern forms when there are lower highs and higher lows, creating converging trendlines.

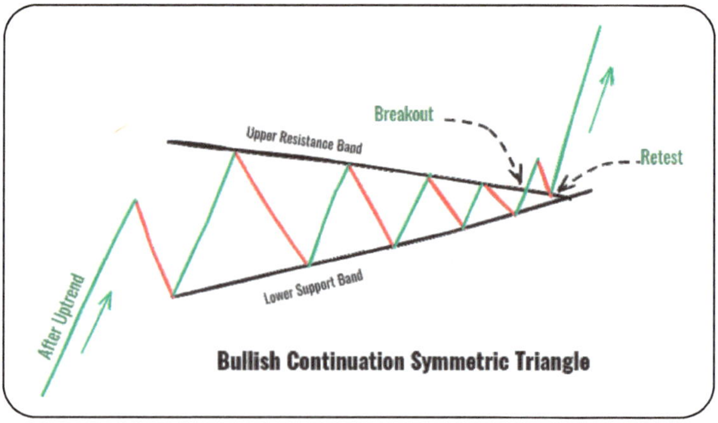

(Fig 7.11)

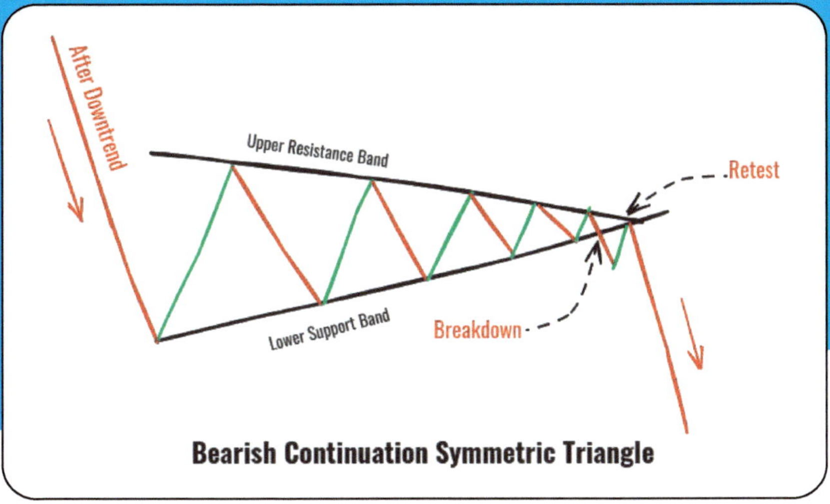

(Fig 7.12)

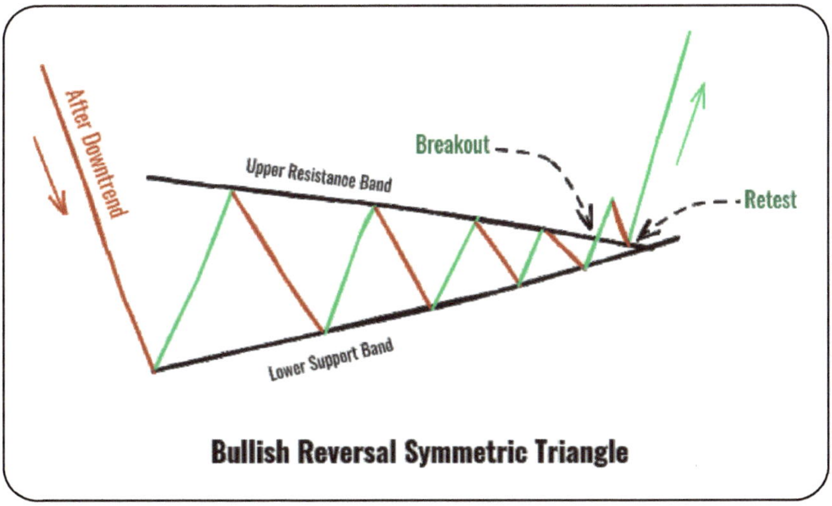

(Fig 7.13)

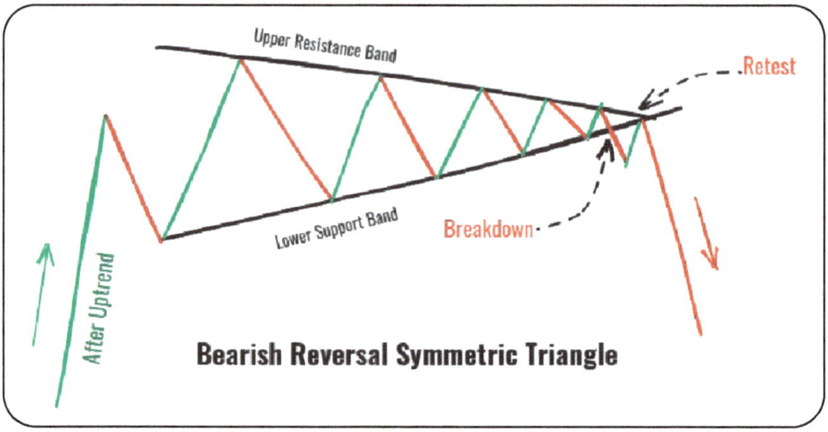

(Fig 7.14)

Symmetrical Triangle Pattern Trade Setup (Fig 7.15 to Fig 7.18):

- **Entry:** A buy or sell signal is generated when the price breaks out above the higher trendline (bullish) or below the lower trendline (bearish).
- **Exit:** The price target is calculated by adding (for bullish breakouts) or subtracting (for bearish breakouts) the vertical height of the triangle at its widest point from the breakout price.
- **Stop Loss:** A stop loss can be placed just inside the triangle opposite the breakout.

While triangle patterns can provide valuable insights into potential price movements, they should not be used in isolation. Considering other technical indicators and the broader market context when using these patterns for trading decisions is essential.

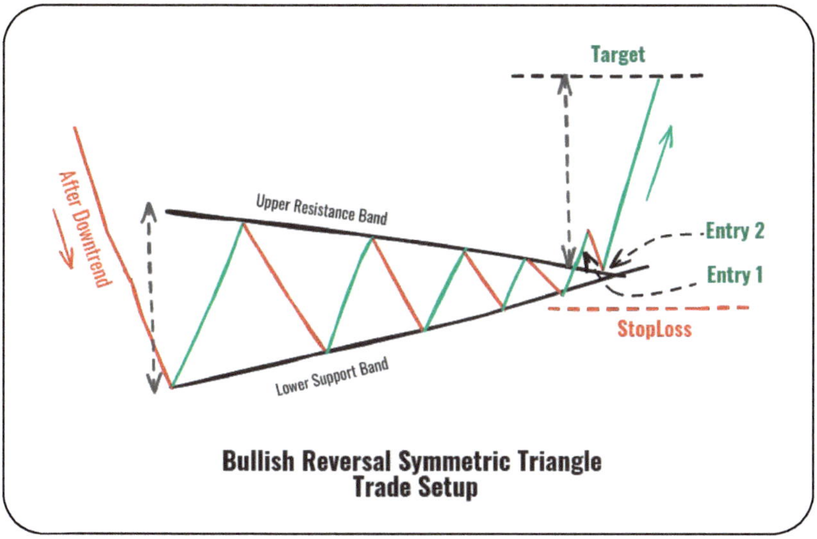

(Fig 7.15)

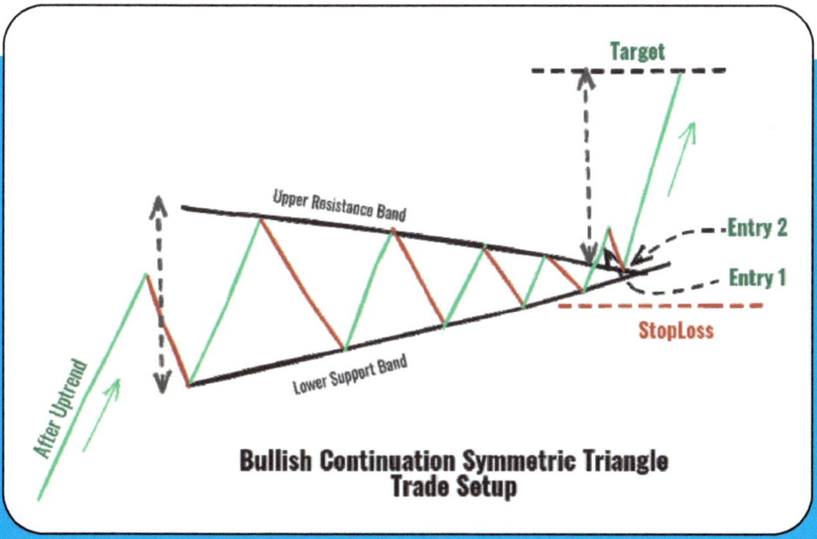

(Fig 7.16)

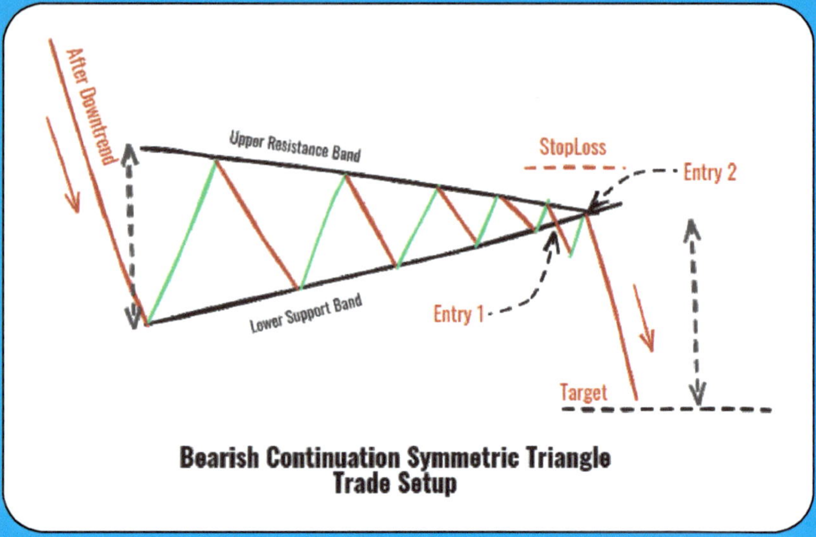

(Fig 7.17)

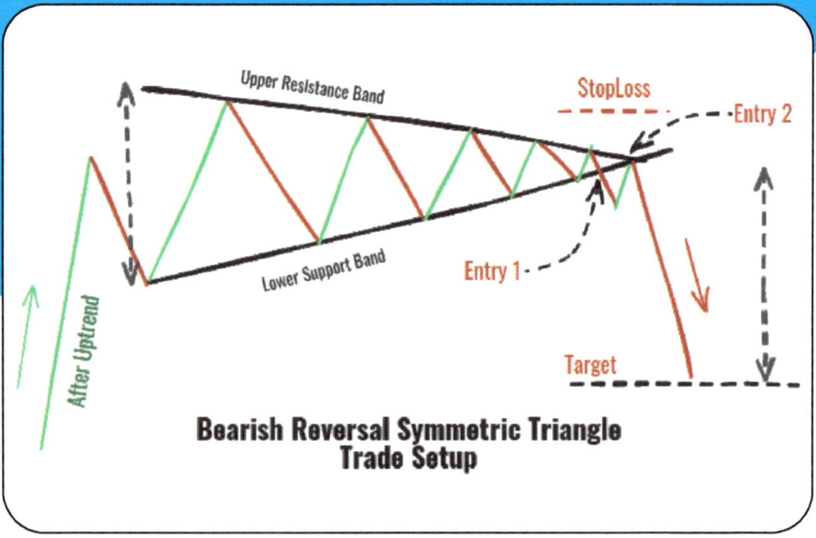

(Fig 7.18)

Case Study 52 : Reliance Industries Ltd.- 2 hr Time rame- 27th July 2020 to 9th September 2020 (Chart 52)

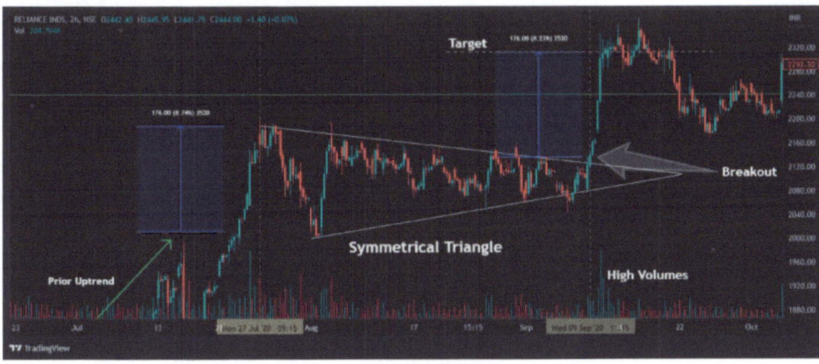

(Chart 52)

Do note that the Symmetrical Triangle pattern is not biased towards breaking upward or downward trendline, and the breakout direction is considered uncertain until it actually occurs. It represents a period of consolidation before the price is forced to breakout or breakdown. A symmetrical triangle can last from a few weeks to many months, unlike the Pennant pattern, which lasts for a short duration only.

7. **Rising Channel / Ascending Parallel Channel :**
   In a Rising Channel, also known as Ascending Parallel Channel, the price oscillates between two upward sloping parallel lines (the channel lines). These lines act as support (lower line) and resistance (upper line) for the price.

Rising Channel Identification checklist (Fig 7.19):

- **Identify the Channel:** First, you need to accurately identify the ascending parallel channel. This channel consists of two parallel lines (upper resistance line and lower support line) with the price oscillating between them. The lines should be sloping upward, indicating a bullish trend.
- **Measure the Channel's Height:** The height of the channel is determined by measuring the vertical distance between the support and resistance lines at the beginning of the channel formation.
- **Calculate the Target Price:** In the event of a breakout, you can calculate the target price by adding the breakout point to the channel's height.

Remember, this is a neutral pattern, so you need to trade as per the context and direction of the breakout.

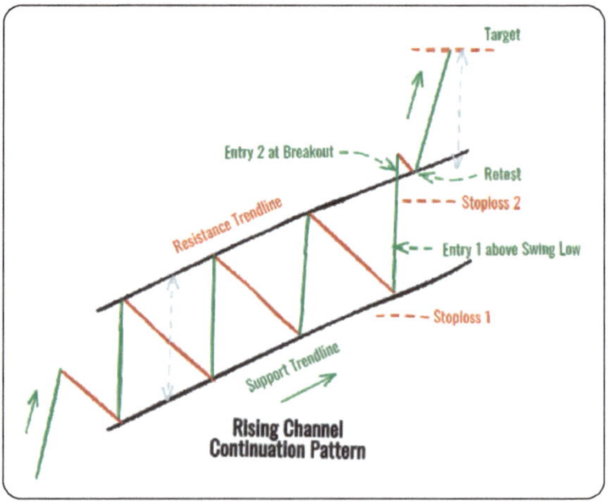

(Fig 7.19)

Rising Channel Pattern Trade Setup (Fig 7.19):

- **Entry**

  Entry 1: Buy at Support level- One common strategy is to buy when the price touches the lower trendline (support). This strategy assumes that the price will rebound from the lower line and rise towards the upper line.

  Entry 2 : Breakout above Resistance level - Some traders might wait for the price to cross the upper trendline (resistance) on a significant volume before entering a long position. This could signal the start of a stronger uptrend.

- **Exit**

  If the price breaks above the resistance line (indicating a continuation of the bullish trend), you would add the height of the channel to the breakout price to estimate the target price & exit accordingly.

- **Stop Loss:**

  The stop loss can be placed just below the support trendline of the channel.

Case Study 53 : Hindustan Aeronautics Limited-Daily Timeframe- 24th Jan 2022 to 5th August 2022 (Chart 53)

(Chart 53)

8. Wedge Pattern :

The Wedge pattern in technical analysis is a continuation or reversal pattern often seen in price charts of financial markets. It is characterized by converging trend lines over a specific period, forming a shape resembling a wedge.

There are two main types of wedge patterns: Rising wedges and Falling wedges.

A. Rising Wedge :

The Rising Wedge (Fig 7.20 and Fig.7.21) is similar to the Ascending Triangle pattern with minor differences.

Unlike the Ascending Triangle, which is a bullish chart pattern, the rising wedge pattern is a bearish chart pattern characterized by a narrowing price range and an upward trend. Both the support and resistance trendlines are sloping upward. But the lower trendline (support) is steeper than the upper line (resistance).

This pattern shows that the highs are climbing more slowly than the lows.

A rising wedge indicates a bearish reversal pattern, typically appearing at the end of an uptrend or a continuation pattern (a pause in the trend) during a downtrend. The bearish signal is confirmed when the price breaks down through the lower trendline.

The rising wedge is a rare and challenging pattern to identify. Although bulls and bears seem to be in relative equilibrium, the rising wedge's shrinking corridor indicates that supply is triumphant. In the end, buyers falter, and sellers seize the initiative.

Rising Wedge Identification Checklist (Fig 7.20 and Fig.7.21) :

- **Uptrend / Downtrend:** Check that the market is in an established uptrend or a prolonged downtrend. The rising wedge can sometimes appear at the end of an uptrend, but it is predominantly a bearish pattern that suggests a reversal of the current trend.
- **Two Converging Trendlines:** Identify two upward-sloping lines that converge as the pattern progresses. The upper trendline represents resistance, and the lower one support.
- **Contracting Range:** Ensure the price range is contracting as the pattern matures. The highs and lows continue to compress until the trading range becomes very narrow compared to the pattern's start.

- **Duration:** A rising wedge can be seen in shorter timeframes like 15 min/ Hourly timeframe or in higher timeframes like Daily or Weekly. The pattern loses its effectiveness over a period much longer than six months.
- **Volume:** Look for declining volume as the pattern progresses, with a spike in volume during the breakout.
- **Breakout:** A confirmation of the pattern is a price breakout, typically to the downside.

Rising Wedge Pattern Trade Setup (Fig 7.20 and Fig 7.21):

- **Entry Point:** Once the pattern is confirmed with a breakout, you can consider shorting the asset or buying a put option if trading options. The ideal entry point for a

  short position is just after the price breaks below the lower trendline of the wedge.
- **Stop Loss:** Set a stop-loss order to manage risk. Depending on your risk tolerance, this could be just above the highest high of the pattern or above the breakout point.
- **Target Price:** The target price is usually determined by subtracting the pattern height from the breakout point. The height of the pattern is the vertical distance between the start of the upper and lower trendlines of the wedge.
- **Monitoring the Trade:** Watch the price action closely after entering the trade. If the price starts to reverse or fails to hit the target price, you may need to adjust your strategy accordingly.

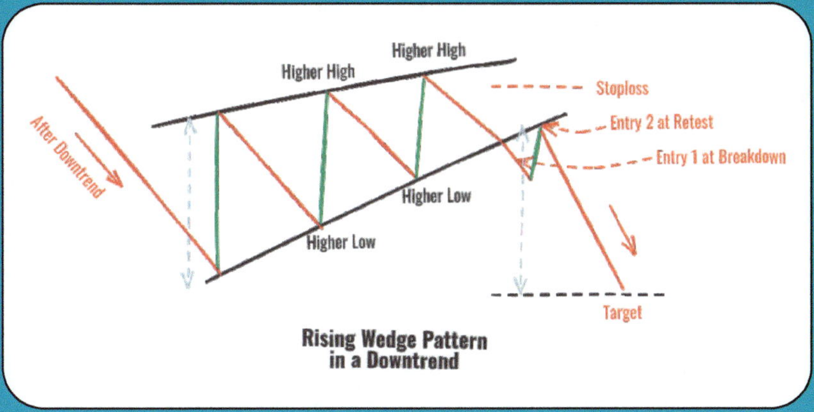

(Fig 7.20)

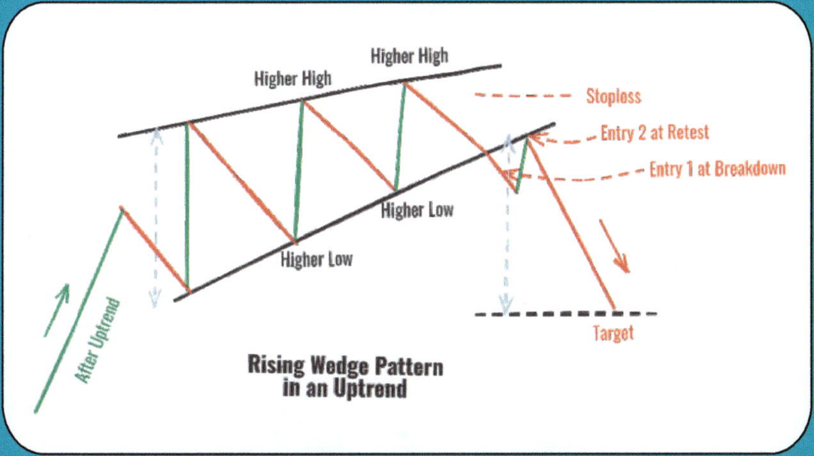

(Fig 7.21)

Case Study 54 : BankNifty- 15 min TimeFrame -18th April 2023 (Chart 54)

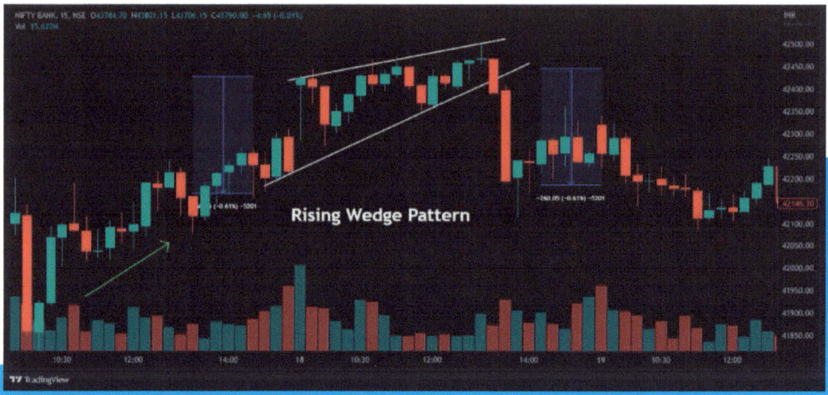

(Chart 54)

B. Falling Wedge:

A falling wedge (Fig 7.22 and Fig.7.23) on the other hand, occurs when the price is trapped between downward-sloping resistance and support lines. Both the highs and the lows are decreasing, but the lows are decreasing faster than the highs. Contrary to the rising wedge, the falling wedge is generally seen as a bullish pattern because it often leads to an upward breakout, indicating a potential reversal of a downtrend.

Falling Wedge Identification Checklist (Fig 7.22 and Fig.7.23):

- **Downtrend:** Ensure that the pattern is forming during a defined downtrend. While falling wedges can sometimes form during uptrends as a bullish continuation pattern, they are primarily seen as reversal patterns.

- **Two Converging Trendlines:** Identify two downward-sloping lines that converge as the pattern progresses. The upper line signifies resistance, and the lower line represents support.
- **Contracting Range:** The pattern should exhibit a contracting range, meaning the highs and lows continue to narrow as the pattern matures.
- **Duration:** A falling wedge can be seen in shorter timeframes like 15 min/ Hourly timeframe or in higher timeframes like Daily or Weekly. The pattern loses its effectiveness over a period much longer than six months.
- **Volume:** Volume typically diminishes as the pattern progresses, with a noticeable increase during the breakout.
- **Breakout:** Confirmation of the pattern comes with a breakout, usually to the upside.

Falling Wedge Pattern Trade Setup (Fig 7.22 and Fig.7.23) :

- **Entry Point:** The ideal 1st entry point for a long position is just after the price breaks out of the upper trendline of the wedge and confirms the pattern. If you're waiting for a pullback or return move, the 2nd entry point would be when the price retests & starts to bounce back from the previously broken trendline.
- **Stop Loss**: A common place to set a stop loss is slightly below the lowest low of the pattern or just below the breakout point, depending on your risk tolerance.

- **Target Price:** The target price is typically calculated by adding the height of the pattern to the breakout point. The height of the pattern is the vertical distance between the start of the upper and lower trendlines of the wedge.
- **Monitoring the Trade:** Watch the price action closely after entering the trade. Adjust your strategy accordingly if the price starts to reverse or fails to hit the target price.

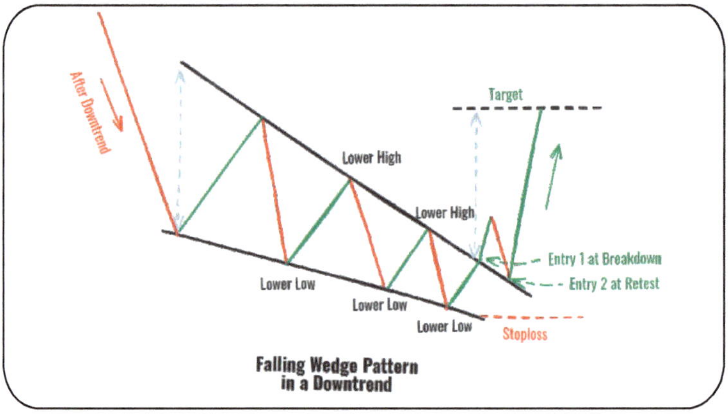

(Fig 7.22)

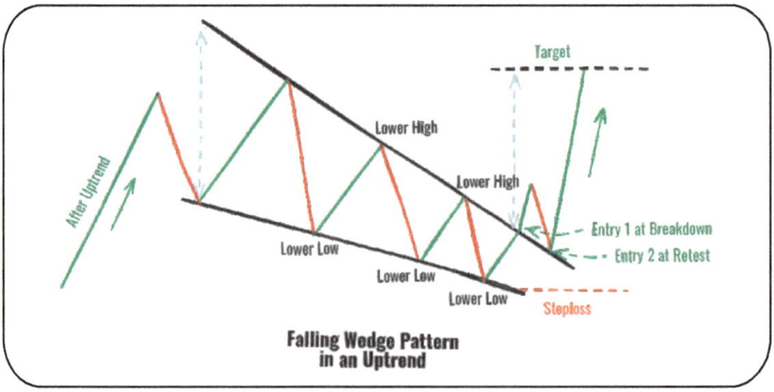

(Fig 7.23)

Case Study 55 : Silver Futures-4Hr Timeframe- 13th July 2022 to 27th July 2022 (Chart 55)

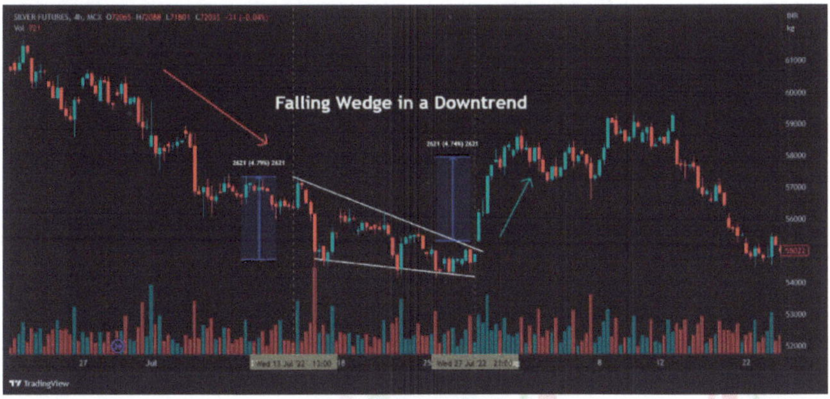

(Chart 55)

9. The Cup & Handle Pattern :

This is a bullish continuation pattern representing a consolidation period followed by a breakout. As the name implies, it resembles a teacup when viewed from the side.

Target of C&H pattern can be 3X or even 5X.

The Cup & Handle Pattern Identification Checklist (Fig 7.24) :

The pattern is comprised of two parts:

- **The Cup:** This is a bowl or rounding bottom-shaped pattern, which forms after an advance. It's a "U" shape and represents a period of consolidation or minor downtrend as sellers push the price down before buyers step back in and the price recovers to the former peak.

- **The Handle:** This is a small downward or sideways drift after the cup, which forms on the right side of the pattern, often in the shape of a flag or pennant. It's typically one-third to one-half the depth of the cup and forms over a shorter period. The handle denotes the final pullback or consolidation before the big breakout.

The Cup & Handle Pattern Trade Setup (Fig 7.24):

- **Entry Point:** The buy signal, or entry point, comes when the price breaks above the resistance line marking the top of the cup (and sometimes the handle). This resistance level is also known as the "lip" of the cup. Traders often set a buy-stop order slightly above this resistance level.
- **Stop-Loss:** To guard against the potential that the breakout fails, a stop-loss order is often placed just below the handle's low.
- Some traders may set it below the right bottom of the cup to allow more room for the stock to fluctuate.
- **Exit Point:** The depth of the cup is equivalent to the predicted price advance after the breakout. So, if the distance from the bottom of the cup to the breakout point is 10 points, then the 1st price target or exit point would be 10 points above the breakout point. Monitoring the stock closely as it approaches this level is essential because it may start to consolidate or reverse.

Remember, like all chart patterns, the Cup and Handle isn't foolproof and doesn't guarantee that the expected price move will occur.

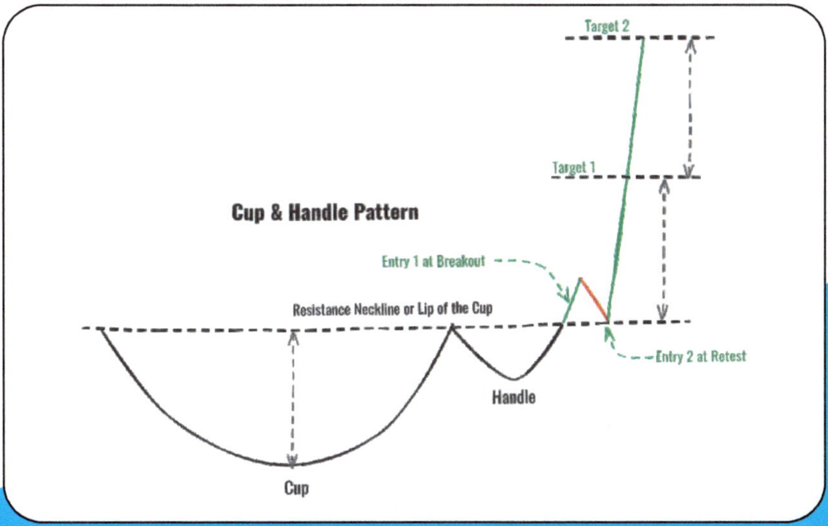

(Fig 7.24)

Cup and Handle Identification checklist

Case Study 56 : Mahindra CIE-Monthly Timeframe-Sep 2018 to Aug 2022 (Chart 56)

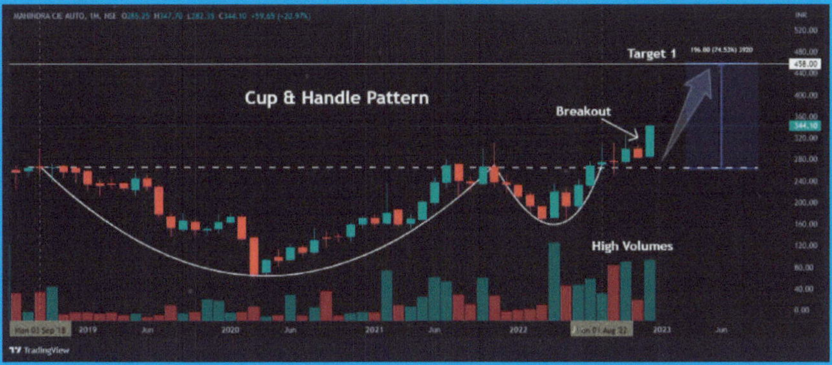

(Chart 56)

Pro Tip : Try to identify C&H pattern on higher timeframes like Monthly or Weekly. It works like wonders.

Case Study 57: Indiabulls Real Estate-Monthly Timeframe-April 2014 to April 2018 (Chart 57)

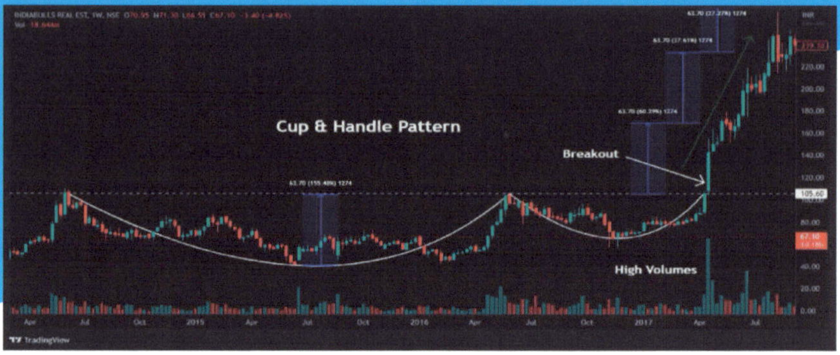

(Chart 57)

Importance of Volume in Breakout Trades:

- **Confirmation of Breakouts:**

  High volume during a breakout is a healthy sign and often suggests a stronger signal. When the price breaches a resistance or support level with a large volume, it means that traders are actively trading at that level. It reinforces the likelihood of the breakout sustaining. If a breakout occurs on low volume, it may be less reliable. It could signal a false breakout, increasing the chance of the price reverting to the previous range.

- **Sustainability of the Trend:**

  High volume on a breakout indicates strong investor interest and momentum, which could drive the price further in the breakout direction. On the contrary, if volume starts to decrease after a breakout, it may suggest that the trend is losing momentum, and a reversal or consolidation might be on the horizon. To sum it up, an increase in volume with a price increase indicates a healthy trend.

Some Pro Tips for trading Chart Patterns :

Trading chart patterns can be a powerful tool for traders. Here are some tips to help new traders master this technique:

1. **Master the Basics First:** Understanding the basic chart patterns like Head & Shoulders, Double Top/Bottom, and various triangle formations is vital. Before moving to more complex patterns, ensure you have a strong grasp of the basics.
2. **Volume Confirmation:** Volume often confirms the validity of a pattern. For instance, during a breakout, a surge in volume is a strong confirmation signal that the pattern is valid.
3. **Wait for Confirmation:** Don't rush to trade the moment you spot a potential pattern. Wait until the pattern is confirmed, often with a breakout or breakdown from the pattern, before entering a position. 80% of the times the neckline will be retested once & you may get a good entry.
4. **Risk/Reward Analysis:** Always calculate the potential risk and reward before taking a trade. The height of the chart pattern can often provide an estimate of the target price, which can be used to analyze the risk/reward.
5. **Not All Patterns Work:** No chart pattern will work 100% of the time. Be prepared for false breakouts or breakdowns and manage your risk accordingly.

6. **Use Multiple Time Frames:** A pattern that appears on a daily chart might not be as significant if the weekly or monthly chart shows a different picture. Confirm patterns on multiple time frames for increased accuracy.

7. **Combine with Other Indicators:** Don't rely solely on chart patterns. Combine them with other tools of technical analysis like trend lines, moving averages, or momentum indicators to improve the accuracy of your trading signals.

8. **Beware of Bias:** It's easy to fall into the trap of seeing patterns that aren't really there because you're biased towards a certain trade outcome. Approach each chart with a neutral perspective.

9. **Practice Makes Perfect:** Practice identifying chart patterns in real time. The more you practice, the better you'll become at spotting them quickly and accurately.

10. **Understand Market Context:** Chart patterns don't form in a vacuum. Always consider the broader market context. If a bullish pattern forms in a bear market, it might not provide a strong trading signal.

11. **Incorporate Price Action:** Understand how price action relates to the formation and confirmation of chart patterns. The behavior of price within the pattern can offer additional clues about its validity.

12. **Use Stop Losses:** Use stop losses to manage risk in case a pattern fails. Stop losses should be placed at a level that confirms the pattern is no longer valid. Remember that you entered a trade because some pattern was formed.

If the SL hits, it's a confirmation that the pattern is no longer valid & you need to move on.

13. **Patterns within Patterns:** Look for smaller patterns forming within larger ones. This can provide early entry opportunities or additional confirmation.

14. **Reversal vs. Continuation:** Understand the difference between reversal and continuation patterns and how to trade them in the context of the prevailing trend.

15. **Breakout Quality Matters:** Not all breakouts are created equal. A strong, high-volume breakout provides a more reliable signal than a weak, low-volume breakout. Also, if the breakout happens after a very long consolidation, consider it to be highly impactful.

16. **Chart Pattern Morphing:** Be aware that one chart pattern can sometimes morph into another. For instance, a failed double top can turn into a head and shoulders pattern.

17. **Don't Ignore the Trend:** The existing trend is critical when trading chart patterns. There is a reason why the trading proverb 'The trend is your friend' is so well-known. Never trade against the trend.

18. **Be Aware of Market Sentiment:** Market sentiment can influence how well chart patterns perform. Awareness of sentiment can help you predict how the price might react after a pattern is formed.

19. **Understand False Breakouts:** False breakouts can often provide trading opportunities.

A failed breakout followed by a breakout in the opposite direction can be a strong trading signal. Sometimes an intentional false breakout is created to remove weak players first, followed by a genuine breakout.

20. **Continuous Learning:** The market is always changing, and so should your knowledge. Never stop learning and adapting your strategies. The stock market is the only place where the journey from being a student to a teacher never ends. Here, wisdom doesn't come with age but with experiences, mistakes, and a never-ending thirst for learning.

As we wrap up this chapter on key price action patterns, let's reflect on what we've learned. These patterns are like the market's own special way of talking to us. They give us clues about what might happen next, helping us make smarter decisions.

Remember, understanding these patterns won't happen in the blink of an eye. It's like learning to decipher a secret code or mastering a new language— it requires time, practice, and, above all, patience. It's about training our eyes to recognize these patterns, and our minds to interpret what they mean for our trading decisions.

As we close this chapter and look forward to the next, remember that every new pattern you learn is another tool in your trading toolbox. And just like building a house, the more tools you have, the better the outcome.

So keep learning, keep practicing, and most importantly, keep trading. Because with every trade, win or lose, is another step on the road to becoming a great trader.

CHAPTER 8
Gaps & Gap Analysis

Gaps, or empty spaces on price charts, indicate instances when no shares were traded inside a specific price range. This typically happens between the market's closing one day and opening the following day.

Up gaps and down gaps are the two main categories of gaps.

After the market closes, the low price must be higher than the day's high price for an upward gap to form. Up gaps are typically thought to be bullish.

A down gap, the opposite of an up gap, occurs when the high price following the market's closing is less than the low price from the previous day. Down gaps are typically viewed as negative or unfavourable.

Why do these Gaps form?

Gaps are caused by unusual buying or selling interests emerging after the market has closed.

A lot of buying interest will be produced overnight, for instance, if an earnings report with unexpectedly strong earnings is released after the market has closed for the day, leading to an imbalance between supply and demand.

The stock's price increases the following day when the market reopens due to the increased demand from investors. An up gap develops if the stock's price stays above its day-ago high for the whole trading session.

The presence of gaps can indicate that the underlying principles or the psychology of the audience that supports this market activity have undergone a significant change.

Timeframe of Gaps:

Up-and-down gaps may appear on daily, weekly, or monthly charts. When they do, they are accompanied by greater than usual volume, which hints that they are significant.

Gaps occur more frequently in the daily timeframe. The gap should occur between Friday's close and Monday's open for weekly charts and between the final day of one month's close and the first day of the following month's open for monthly charts. Gaps on weekly or monthly charts are relatively uncommon.

Four main categories of Gaps:

1. Common Gap
2. Breakaway Gap
3. Runaway Gap
4. Exhaustion Gap

1. **Common Gaps:**

   They are also referred to as Trading Gaps or Area Gaps. Typically, the common gap is uneventful. They may even result from a stock going ex-dividend when there is little activity in the market.

   Low trading volume is another characteristic of this gap. Understanding these common gaps is helpful. Still, when these gaps are seen, one should not expect any trading opportunities in the market.

2. **Breakaway Gaps:**

   Typically, the breakaway gap appears at the end of a significant price pattern and indicates a significant market movement. These gaps happen whenever the price action breaks a trading range or congestion zone.

   Understanding the characteristics of market congestion locations is necessary to comprehend these gaps. A Congestion area is nothing but a price range in which the market has been trading for some time, often a few weeks or even more. When approached from below, the region around the top of the congestion area typically presents resistance. When viewed from above, the region close to the bottom of the congested area serves as support.

   Market enthusiasm and a large volume of buyers relative to sellers for upside breakouts or a large number of sellers relative to buyers for downside breakouts are necessary for these gaps to be formed. If I see a breakaway gap in high volume, I might consider it a signal of the start of a new trend.

Case Study 58: IDFC First Bank-Daily Timeframe-2nd May 2023 (Chart 58)

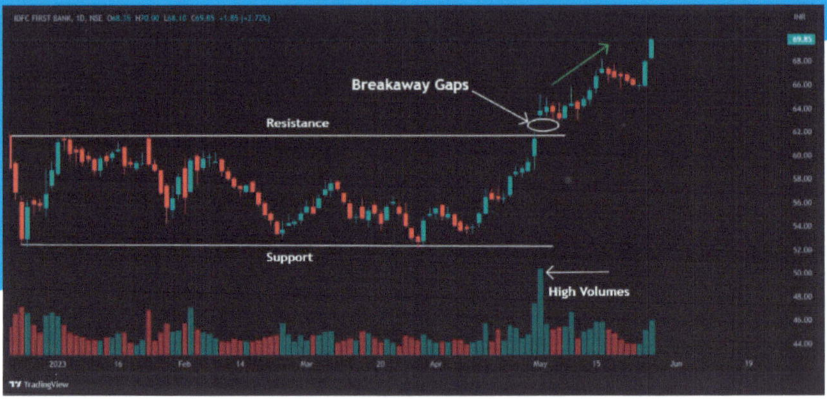

(Chart 58)

Case Study 59: IDFC Bank-Daily Timeframe-1st August 2022 (Chart 59)

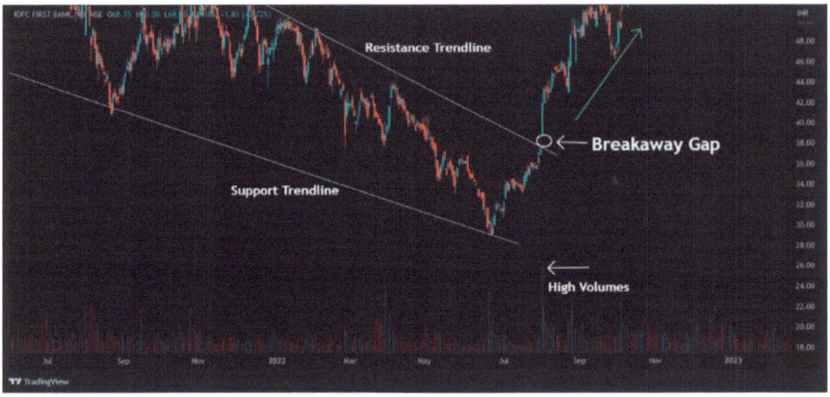

(Chart 59)

3. **Runaway or Continuation Gaps:**

   Runaway gaps are best characterized as gaps brought on by rising stock interest. Runaway gaps to the upside often signify traders who missed the uptrend's original entry point and who, after watching for a price correction, determined it would not occur. Suddenly, there is an increase in buying interest, and the price soars over the closing of the previous day. Runaway gaps of this nature signify traders on the verge of panic.

   Additionally, a strong uptrend may experience runaway gaps from important news stories that spark renewed interest in the stock.

Case Study 60: Nifty50 Index -Daily Timeframe July - August 2022 (Chart 60)

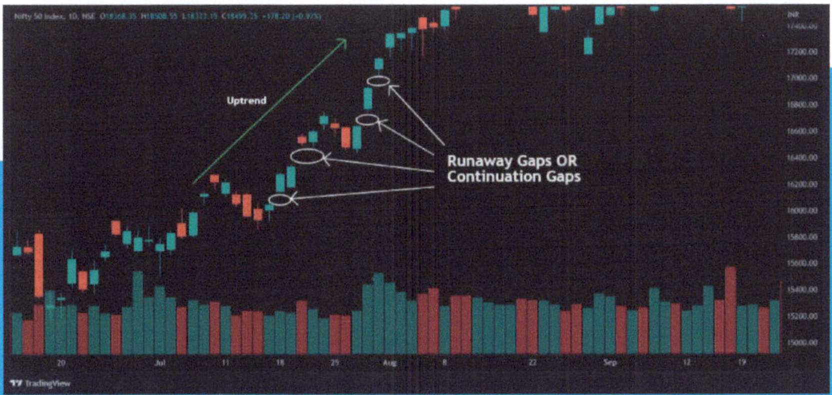

(Chart 60)

4. **Exhaustion Gaps:**

Exhaustion gaps occur at the tail end of a strong up or downtrend. They frequently serve as the first clue that a move has finished. High volume and a significant price differential between the previous day's closing and the new opening price help to identify them. If the very high volume is not noticed, they can be misconstrued as runaway gaps.

As prices change direction, exhaustion gaps are easily filled.

Similarly, if they occur during an uptrend, traders experience bullish euphoria, and buyers become enamoured with that stock. Huge volume price gaps are followed by massive profit-taking, and the stock's demand completely disappears. Prices fall, and the trend dramatically shifts.

After this gap, one can wait for signals showing that the trend is losing momentum or reversing. **This could be in the form of candlestick patterns such as a Hanging Man, a Shooting Star, a Doji at the top of an uptrend or a Hammer or a Doji in a downtrend.**

One trick for identifying these gaps is that, during uptrends, it is not followed by new highs, and in the case of downtrends, it is not followed by new lows. However, it is confirmed only when prices reverse and fill it.

Case Study 61: Nifty50 Index Daily Timeframe 21st December 2022 (Chart 61)

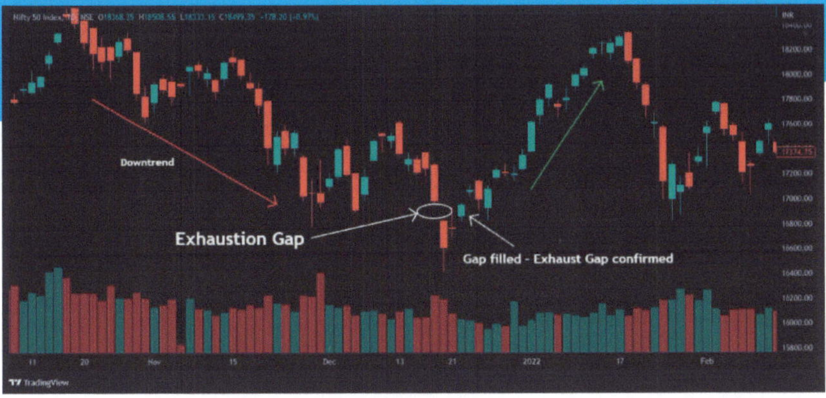

(Chart 61)

Remember, even if an exhaustion gap is identified correctly, it does not guarantee that the price will change direction. Like all aspects of technical analysis, one should use exhaustion gaps with other indicators and analysis techniques.

A common stock trading saying is, **"All gaps get filled."** However, it's not a hard rule and depends on the type of gap and overall market conditions. While common gaps and exhaustion gaps often get filled as prices revert to previous levels, breakaway and continuation gaps may not be filled for a long time as they often accompany strong trends.

Here are some Gap Trading Strategies :

1. **A breakaway gap:** Sell short and place a stop a few ticks above the gap's upper rim.
2. **An exhaustion gap:** Prices pull back into it the next day: The downtrend is over: Cover shorts immediately.
3. **A continuation gap in a downtrend:** Go short, stopping a few ticks above the upper rim of the gap.
4. **An exhaustion gap** closed two days after it opened: Cover shorts immediately.
5. **A common gap** amid a congestion area closed the next day: No action is recommended.
6. **A breakaway gap:** Go long and set a stoploss a few ticks below the lowest rim of the gap.
7. **A continuation gap:** Add to longs and place a trailing stop-loss a few ticks below the gap's lower rim. Either a continuation gap or an exhaustion gap could exist near the right edge of the chart. Relatively quiet volume suggests continuation. If you buy, place a protective stop-loss a few ticks below the lower rim of this gap.

The above seven strategies are not mine.

It is the sole property of professional trader Dr Alexander Elder.

Some Pro Tips for Trading Gaps :

Trading gaps can be profitable but also quite challenging. Here are some tips to help you trade better :

1. **Differentiate Gap Types:** Understand the different types of gaps, such as Common, Breakaway, Runaway (Measuring), and Exhaustion gaps, as discussed in this chapter. Each has different implications and trading strategies.
2. **Volume is Important:** The volume on the gap day can provide important clues. A high-volume gap is more likely to signify a strong, potentially sustainable move.
3. **Watch the Fill:** Many gaps will eventually "fill" or return to their pre-gap prices. Knowing when a gap might fill can be helpful, but don't assume every gap will fill quickly. Do note that Gaps act as resistance as well.
4. **Use Other Technical Indicators:** Combine gap analysis with other technical indicators to confirm signals and refine your trading decisions.
5. **Recognize Continuation Patterns:** Gaps can often form as part of continuation patterns (like Runaway gaps). Recognize these patterns for potential trading opportunities.
6. **Be Aware of Earnings Dates:** Earnings reports often cause price gaps. Be aware of when companies you trade are releasing earnings.
7. **Mind the Trend:** Gaps are often more significant when they occur in the direction of the trend. A gap in the direction of the trend could signal continuation. In contrast, a gap against the trend could indicate a potential reversal.

8. **Analyze Gap Size:** The size of the gap can provide clues. Large gaps are more likely to signal a strong move, while small gaps might just be noise.
9. **Beware of False Breakouts:** Like chart patterns, gaps can lead to false breakouts. Always manage your risk.
10. **Gap & Go Strategy:** Consider the "gap and go" strategy, where you trade in the direction of the gap at market open.
11. **Use Stop-Loss Orders:** Always use stop-loss orders when trading gaps. If the price moves against you, this can help you minimize your losses.
12. **Wait for Confirmation:** Wait for some confirmation before trading a gap. This could be a specific candlestick pattern, a breakout from a certain price level, or a confirmation from another technical indicator.
13. **Practice Patience:** Be patient when trading gaps. Not every gap presents a viable trading opportunity.
14. **Gap Zones:** Understand the concept of gap zones (support/resistance levels created by gaps). These can act as a target or stop levels for your trades.
15. **Trading the Gap Fill:** Consider trading strategies that profit from a gap filling. This involves shorting a stock after a gap up or buying after a gap down, anticipating that the price will return to its pre-gap level.
16. **Use Multiple Time Frames:** Confirm gaps on multiple time frames to ensure they are significant.

17. **Understand Market Sentiment:** Market sentiment can influence gap formations. Bullish sentiment could lead to continued price rises after a gap up. In contrast, bearish sentiment could lead to continued falls after a gap down.

18. **Check the News:** Common Gaps often occur because of domestic & international news events. Always check the news to understand what might have caused the gap.

19. **Risk/Reward Analysis:** Like any trade, analyze the potential risk and reward before trading a gap.

20. **Continuous Learning:** Always keep learning. The more you understand gaps and how they interact with other aspects of technical analysis, the better your trading will be.

As we end this chapter on Gaps and Gap analysis, let's take a moment to appreciate the crucial role these patterns play in our trading journey. Gaps, these seemingly silent spaces, can indeed be loud narrators of the market story if only we learn to listen. They are like signposts on our investment highway, providing vital clues about where the market could be headed.

It's important to remember that understanding gaps isn't a piece of cake—it's like learning to read a hidden script. But we can get a handle on it with consistent practice and patience. Just as detective pieces together various clues to solve a mystery, a trader uses gap analysis to decode the probable market's intentions.

So, keep your eyes open for these gaps. They might appear empty, but they are filled with valuable information. As we close this chapter and move to the next, let's carry forward this knowledge, knowing that with each gap we analyze, we will be one step closer to becoming better, more informed traders.

CHAPTER 9
How to Use Candlesticks More Effectively

As seen in the previous chapters, candlesticks provide a visual representation of price action over a specified period of time and can be used to gain more information about market trends, sentiment and potential trading opportunities.

Here are some ways to get more information from candlesticks:

Candlesticks are the most popular form of financial chart used to display the price movement of an asset. To get more information from candlesticks, you can look at the following:

1. **Candlestick Patterns:**

   Identifying specific patterns such as Doji, Hammer and others at important levels can provide insight into market sentiment and future price movement. We will understand Doji in the upcoming section.

2. **Candlestick Colors:**

   The color of a candlestick (green or red) indicates whether the closing price was higher or lower than the opening price.

3. **Body Size:**
   The size of the candlestick body represents the difference between the opening and closing prices, and a long body can indicate strong buying or selling pressure.

4. **Shadows:**
   The length of the upper and lower shadows can indicate the high and low prices for the period and show how much the price moved.

5. **Volume:**
   The volume associated with a candlestick can provide additional information about market sentiment and the strength of price moves.

Additionally, combining candlesticks with other technical analysis tools, such as moving averages or trend lines, can provide a more comprehensive picture of market trends and price movements.

It's important to keep in mind that candlestick analysis is just one tool among many that traders and investors can use to make informed decisions, and that no single indicator can provide a complete picture of market activity. By combining multiple indicators and techniques, traders and investors can get a more comprehensive view of market conditions and potential trading opportunities.

In the next section, we will see in detail how certain candlestick patterns can provide vital information about market sentiment.

Doji :

Neutral candlesticks are candlesticks that do not have a strong bullish or bearish bias, and can indicate indecision between buyers and sellers in the market. In a market with a strong trend, neutral candlesticks can indicate that the trend may be losing momentum and that a reversal may be imminent. In a market with limited price movement, neutral candlesticks can indicate that the market is in a period of consolidation, and that a breakout may be imminent in either direction.

Doji is a neutral candlestick pattern.

In technical analysis, it is used to identify potential changes in the market trend. It is formed when the opening and closing prices of a security are roughly the same, resulting in a small body with long upper and lower shadows. This indicates that, during the time frame represented by the candlestick, the market was in a state of indecision, with prices fluctuating and then closing near the opening price.

A Doji can signal a potential reversal in the market trend and is often considered a bearish or bullish reversal pattern depending on preceding price action and future price movements.

If every candle is a tug of war between the Bulls & Bears, then Doji candles signify a match that ends in a draw (Fig 9.1).

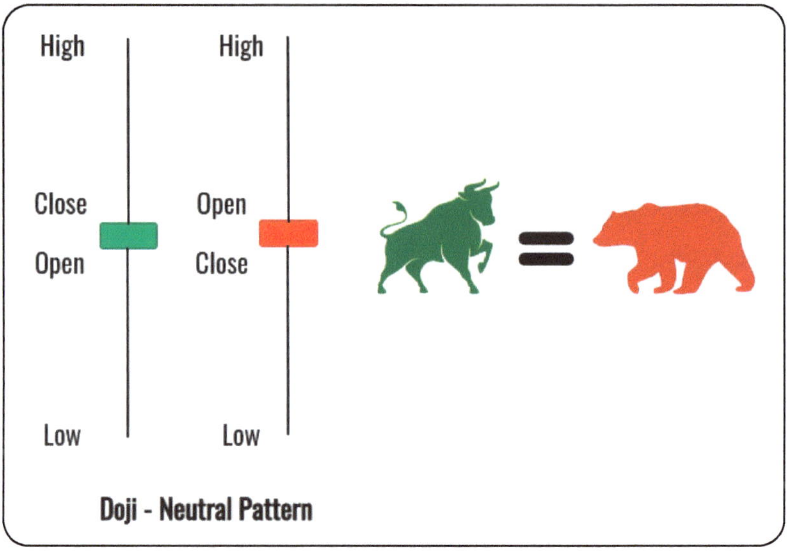

(Fig 9.1)

Dojis (chart 62 & chart 63) are symbols representing ambiguity. Dojis are smaller, both in terms of their true bodies and their upper and lower shadows.

However, it is important to consider other technical and fundamental factors before making a trading decision based on a Doji pattern.

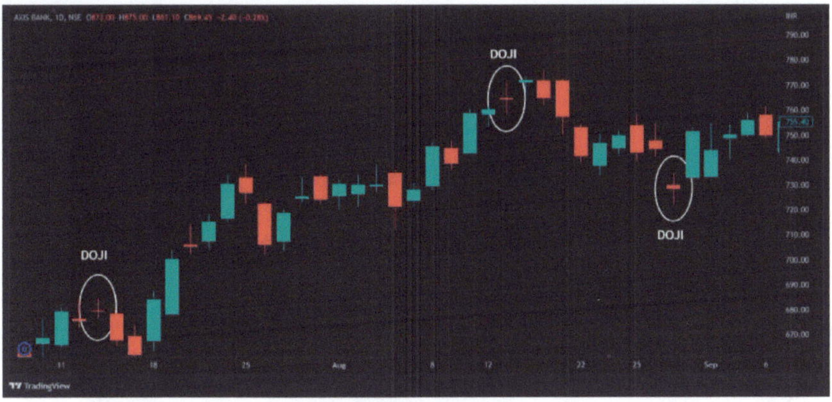

(Chart 62)

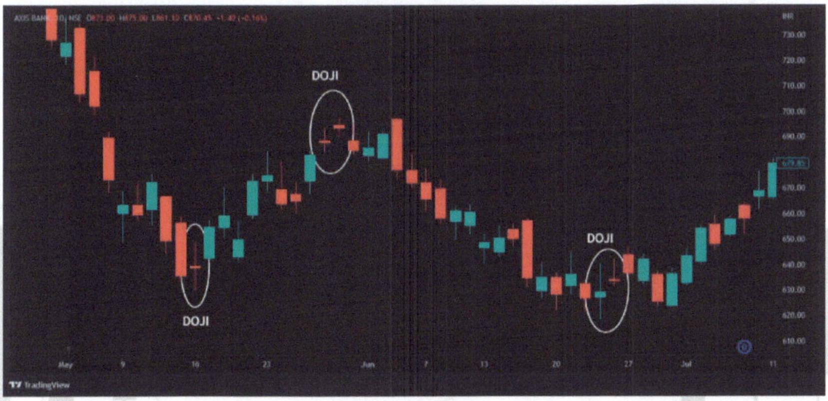

(Chart 63)

On the charts, when you see extra long shadows of the candles, such patterns are called Rejection patterns. Bullishness or Bearishness can be decided as per the location of the actual body.

Bullish Rejection Patterns :

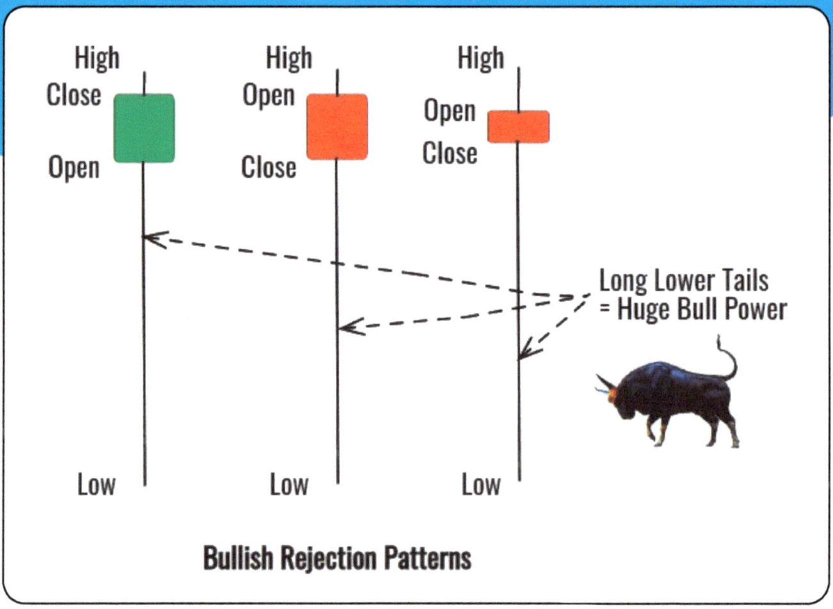

(Fig 9.2)

Check out chart 64 and chart 65 to understand how a Bullish Rejection pattern looks.

(Chart 64)

(Chart 65)

Do make a note that *no chart pattern in technical analysis works 100% of the time.* Chart patterns are just one aspect of technical analysis, and their accuracy can be influenced by various factors such as market conditions, news events and investor sentiment.

Bearish Rejection Patterns :

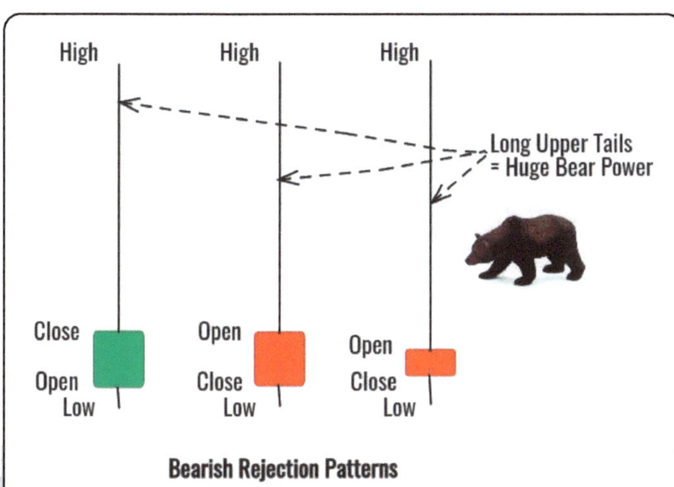

(Fig 9.3)

Look at chart 66 and chart 67 to understand how a Bearish Rejection pattern looks.

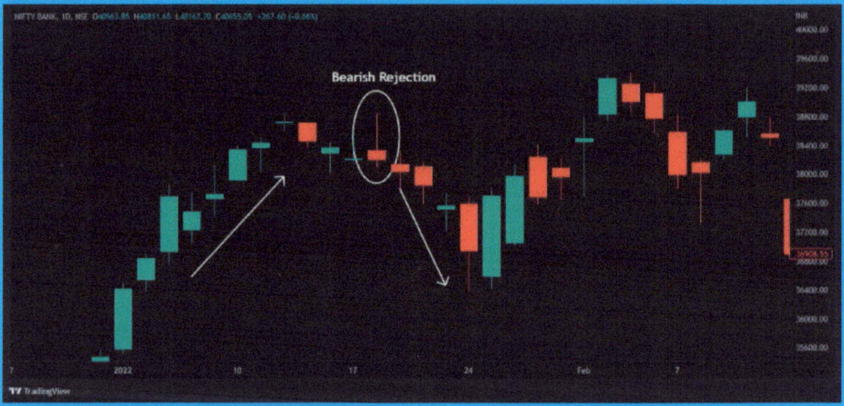

(Chart 66)

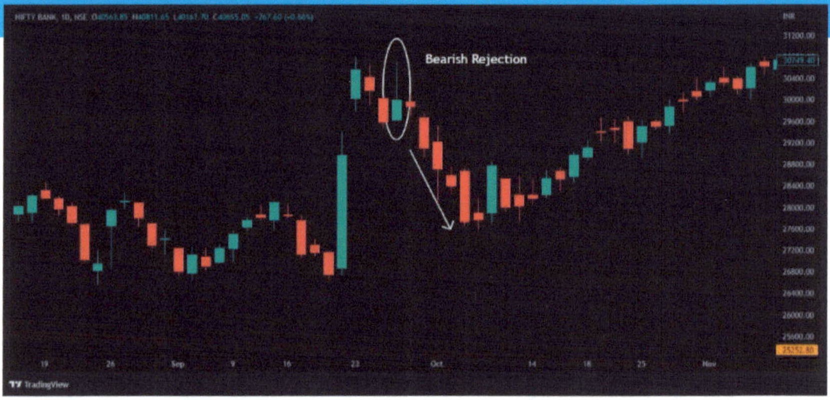

(Chart 67)

Giant Sized Candlesticks :

Asking yourself "What's the size of the candlestick pattern related to the earlier ones ? " will help you determine the strength of a move.

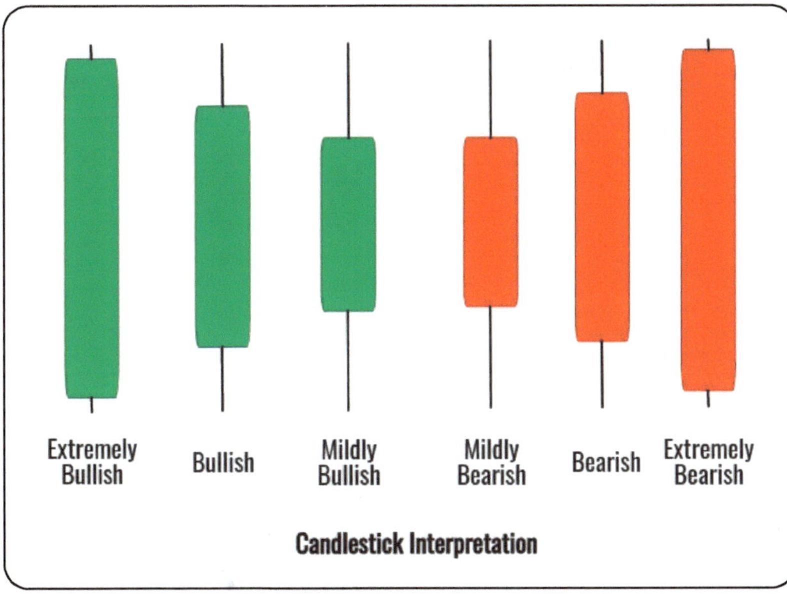

(Fig 9.4)

Look at chart 68 where you will find all the discussed candlesticks

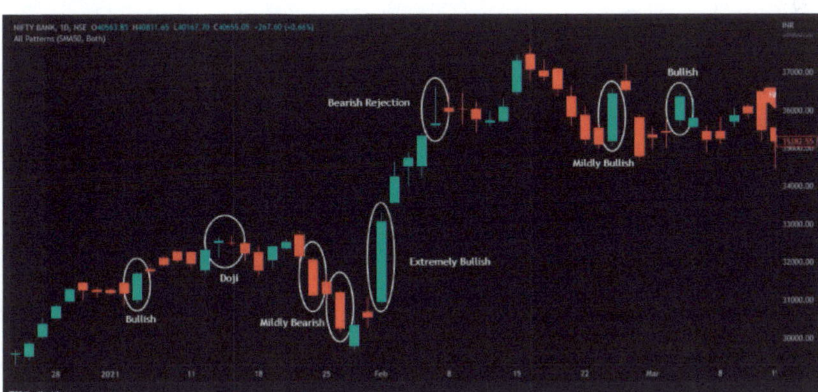

(Chart 68)

Takeaways:

- More important than the pattern's type is where the candlestick pattern appears.
- Before making any trade decision, wait until the candlestick has fully formed.
- Know the trend first, and then look for a reversal indication.
- For any chart, it is important to analyze the higher timeframe first.
- Wait for a follow-up candle or confirmation candle once a candlestick pattern has formed.

CHAPTER 10
Smart Money & Advanced Volume Analysis

Volume is one of market analysis's most crucial yet often overlooked aspects. In its simplest terms, Volume refers to the total number of shares or contracts traded in a security or market during a given period. But it's not just about raw numbers; Volume can provide traders with a deep understanding of the liquidity and activity levels of a specific market or security.

The term 'Smart Money' refers to institutional investors, hedge funds, and other financial professionals with a track record of making profitable investments. These entities tend to have more resources, experience, and information than retail investors. Thus, their actions are closely watched in the financial markets.

In the context of Smart Money - the institutional investors, professional traders, hedge funds, and other experienced market participants - volume analysis becomes even more critical. This is because Smart Money can significantly impact Volume due to the size of their transactions. When these significant market players take positions or initiate trades, they leave footprints in the form of volume spikes, climaxes, and divergences. By analyzing Volume, we can gain valuable insights into what Smart Money might be doing.

Let's get familiar with a few key terms connected to volume.

1. **Volume Spikes :**
   A sudden increase in trading volume often suggests Smart Money activity. It could indicate a new position being established or an existing one being liquidated. Traders should note the price action associated with volume spikes – a surge in Volume during a price rise might indicate strong buying interest. In contrast, a volume spike during a price decline could signify strong selling pressure.

Case Study 69: JBM Auto Ltd. Weekly Timeframe 30th January 2023 (Chart 69)

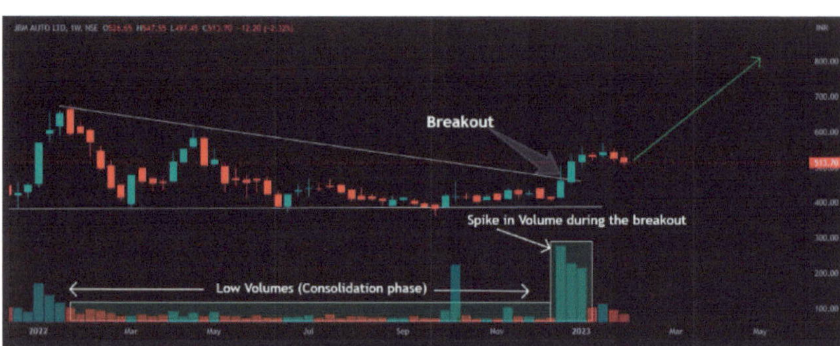

(Chart 69)

Here, in Chart 69 of JBM Auto Ltd., it can be seen that before the breakout happened, there was an entire year where trading happened with fewer volumes. Then you suddenly come across a volume spike which indicates that Smart Money has entered. When writing this book, JBM Auto Ltd. is trading at INR 513/-.

Let's see where Smart Money takes this stock in future.

2. Volume Climaxes:

Volume climaxes occur when Volume reaches an exceptionally high level relative to recent activity, often at the peak of price trends. A buying climax (high Volume on an up day) may suggest Smart Money is selling or distribution is happening, signalling a potential market top. A selling climax (high Volume on a down day) might mean Smart Money is buying or accumulation is taking place, indicating a possible market bottom.

3. Volume and Price Divergence:

Divergence between price and Volume can provide key insights. Suppose prices are rising while Volume is falling. In that case, it might suggest a lack of conviction from Smart Money and could signal a potential price reversal. Conversely, suppose prices are falling, and Volume is diminishing. In that case, it may indicate decreased selling pressure and hint at a possible upward turn.

4. **On-Balance Volume (OBV) Indicator:**

   The On-Balance Volume (OBV) indicator measures cumulative buying and selling pressure by adding Volume on "up" days and subtracting Volume on "down" days. A technical analysis indicator, OBV measures the cumulative flow of Volume in relation to a stock's price movement.

   The idea behind OBV is that Volume is a crucial driver of price changes and that changes in Volume can signal changes in price direction. For example, if the Volume is increasing significantly while the price remains steady, it could indicate that the price is about to move upward. It can help identify when Smart Money is flowing into or out of a stock. If OBV is flat while prices are rising, it could suggest that Smart Money is currently losing interest in the stock & a probable reversal is on the cards.

   The idea behind OBV is that Volume precedes price, so a rising OBV line can potentially signal an upward trend in price. In contrast, a falling OBV line can potentially signal a downward trend in price.

Here's are the steps to read the OBV indicator:

1. **Identify the OBV line on your chart:** The OBV is usually displayed as a line chart below your price chart.
2. **Analyze the direction of the OBV line:** If the OBV line is rising, it means that Volume is heavier on up days. This could be a sign of intense buying pressure, which might indicate an upward trend in price. If the OBV line is falling, it means that Volume is heavier on down days, which could be a sign of intense selling pressure and might indicate a downward trend in price.

3. **Compare the OBV trend to the price trend:** If the price is rising and the OBV is also rising, this is usually considered bullish. It indicates that buying volume is supporting the price increase. On the other hand, if the price is falling and the OBV is also falling, this is usually considered bearish, indicating that the selling Volume is supporting the price decrease.

4. **Look for divergences:** Divergences between price and OBV can provide potential reversal signals. For instance, if the price is rising, but OBV is falling, it might suggest that the upward trend is losing strength and could be about to reverse. Conversely, if the price is falling, but OBV is rising, it might suggest that the downward trend is losing strength and could be about to reverse.

Case Study 70: Infosys Ltd. Weekly Timeframe January 2021 to January 2022 (Chart 70)

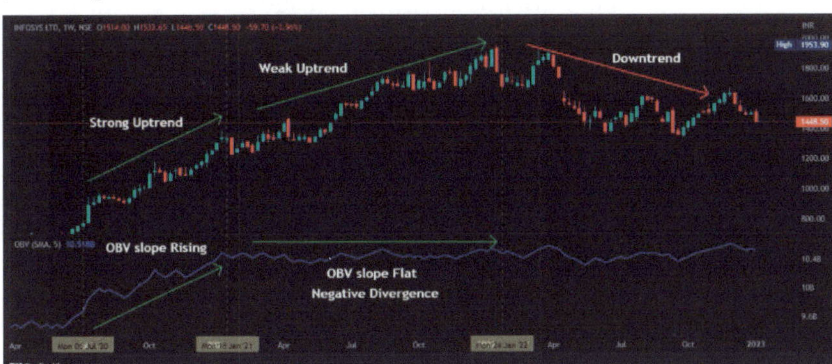

(Chart 70)

As can be seen in Chart 70, both price action and OBV indicator were initially moving upwards, indicating a strongly rising trend. Since January 2021, the OBV has been nearly flat while the price has continued to rise and reach new highs. This resulted in negative divergence, indicating that Smart Money is losing interest in the stock, implying that there may be a reversal or that the short-term upswing is ending.

Keep in mind that the actual value of the OBV is unimportant; instead, focus on its direction.

PRO TIPS

(Keep them in mind while using the OBV indicator)

1. The rising trend is expected to continue when both price and OBV have higher peaks and lower bottoms.
2. The negative trend is expected to continue when both price and OBV make lower peaks and lower troughs.
3. If the OBV rises during a trading range, accumulating may occur, signalling an impending upward breakout.
4. If the OBV falls during a trading range, distribution may occur, signalling a downward breakout.
5. When the price continues to rise and the OBV fails to rise, the upward trend will likely stagnate or fail. This is known as a negative divergence.
6. The negative trend is likely to continue when the price continues to create lower troughs, but OBV does not.

Advanced Volume Analysis :

A key market analysis component is Volume, which is the quantity of shares or contracts traded in a security or market over a specific period.

It offers a window into the strength or weakness of a market move. It provides traders with insights that go beyond price action alone.

Volume analysis is a complex field, and it's essential to interpret volume data in the proper context. When used in conjunction with price action analysis and other technical indicators, Volume can provide valuable insights into the behaviour of Smart Money. However, traders should remember that volume analysis, like all forms of market analysis, isn't foolproof and should form only one part of a comprehensive trading strategy.

Volume and Trend Confirmation:

Volume can confirm how strong a trend is. Volume should increase in a rising market. To keep driving prices higher, buyers must continue to buy in greater quantities and with greater enthusiasm. A warning sign that the trend might shift is an increase in pricing and a decrease in Volume, both of which point to a lack of interest.

Volume and Market Reversals:

High volumes often characterize market tops. If there's a sudden and heavy volume during the phase of price advance, it can be a sign that this trend is about to reverse. This is because such a situation may indicate that the market is overbought.

Volume Oscillators:

These are tools derived from volume data to help identify when markets are overbought or oversold. Examples include the On Balance Volume (OBV) indicator, which we have already discussed in detail.

Conclusion :

As we wrap up this chapter on Smart Money and advanced volume analysis, let's remember that mastering these techniques isn't a sprint but a marathon. It takes time, patience, and a good dose of perseverance to decode the intricate dance of smart money and the subtle signals revealed through volume analysis. It's like learning to read a new language or play a musical instrument—you won't be an expert overnight. But remember every step forward, no matter how small, brings us closer to our goal.

Just as every seasoned sailor was once a novice who had to learn how to navigate the high seas, every expert trader started as a beginner, puzzled by the market's ups and downs. But they didn't give up. And neither should you. Every challenging market situation is a new opportunity to learn and grow. As we continue this journey, let's take heart from the fact that with time, patience, and diligence, we willl understand the market's signals, predict its moves, and sail smoothly through its choppy waters. So keep learning, keep practicing, and above all, keep going. The road to mastery is long, but the view from the top is worth it.

CHAPTER 11

Money Management & Trading Psychology

"I fear not the man who has practiced 10,000 kicks once, but I fear the man who has practiced one kick 10,000 times." - Bruce Lee

In this book, I've concentrated only on a few of the candlestick patterns that successful traders frequently use. I wholeheartedly concur with what the late Bruce Lee said. It is more than enough to have a good trading career if you can merely master a few patterns.

One needs money to stay alive, fight another battle and win another trade.

Money management is not just about putting stop losses but also about position sizing.Knowing how much to buy is as important as knowing how much to risk.

Trading is not gambling & neither should it be treated as such.

Risk in the trading business is inevitable, but one can control the amount of risk by controlling the bet size on each trade.Proper money management will always ensure that you only bet within your risk capacity.

Stop losses are the vital elements of the trading business & must always be taken with pride, as it is the only friend of a trader in a war of Bulls & Bears.

A Drawdown (loss) can really DRAW YOU DOWN beyond imagination.

The following table (Table 11.1) shows the returns you will need to generate after various drawdowns to return to the original capital or break even.

Loss % per Trade	% Returns required for breakeven
1%	1%
5%	5.3%
10%	11.1%
15%	17.6%
20%	25%
25%	33%
30%	43%
50%	100%
60%	150%
70%	300%
80%	900%

(Table 11.1)

Let's examine this idea more thoroughly:

Let's say you have bought a stock of Rs. 100.

Let's say the stock price drops by 50% over a long period of time.

Thus, the stock price now is at Rs. 50.

Assume once more that the stock price has risen by 50%.

In light of this, the new stock price is Rs. 75.

Keep in mind that you are still down by 25% compared to the initial pricing of Rs. 100/-.

Always remember that a stock that goes down by 50% and again goes up by 50% is still down by 25%.

If you incur a significant loss in a particular trade, your available trading capital decreases by a certain percentage. Therefore, you must recover this loss before you can gain overall profits. Thus, the more significant the loss, the larger the returns required to bring it back to breakeven, which is evident from table 11.1.

To conclude, controlling the damage & limiting losses is better than running after recoveries. So taking stop loss is necessary in case a trade fails.

Money management & Position Sizing :

Money management is a critical aspect of successful trading and involves making smart decisions about how to allocate and manage your trading capital. Risk management is essential to determine the amount of risk you are willing to take in each trade and stick to it. A good rule of thumb is to not risk more than 2% of your capital in a single trade. However since some of the stocks are volatile & may take your 2% stop loss early, I recommend keeping the acceptable risk at 5% per trade. This means **you can lose only a maximum 5% of your capital per trade, if you are wrong.**

Proper position sizing helps you manage your risk and keep your trading capital intact. The size of your position should be based on the amount of capital you have and the amount of risk you are willing to take.

Position Sizing calculation :

$$\text{Position Sizing} = \frac{\text{Total Permissible Risk in Rs.}}{\text{Stop Loss in Points}}$$

Now let us apply all the ideas from this book to a real-world trade.

Let's say your trading account has 2 lakhs in it and you decide to put the entire sum into Reliance Industries Ltd. stock. According to our policy, the greatest risk we may accept is 5%.

Remember from Table 11.1 that you need to produce a profit

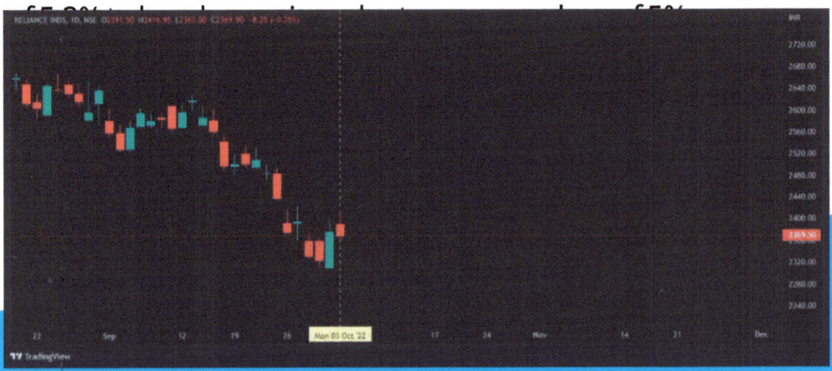

(Chart 71)

Refer chart 50. On 3rd October 2022, Reliance Industries Ltd. was trading at Rs. 2,365/-. Also you were able to spot the Bullish Engulfing pattern formed in the daily timeframe on the chart. By money management rules, you want to risk only 5% of your capital in this trade. So now ideally you have two stop-losses in mind.

Sl1 - It is 5% of the entry point 2365 which comes out to be 2252
SL2 - It is kept at the lowest low point of the Bullish engulfing pattern as we have discussed in Chapter no. 3. Note that this is also a very tight stoploss of approximately 3% from the entry price.

Both the stoplosses are completely okay & are as per money management rules.

After you have finished reading this book, please send me an email at **stocksinvader@gmail.com** with your feedback. I would be happy to share the Position Sizing calculator (as shown in the below image) with you for free. This calculator will tell you how many shares to buy each time based on the risk amount you enter.

Position Size Calc using SL Price	
Enter your Risk amount in ₹	10000
Enter Buying Price	2365
Enter StopLoss Price	2252
Your Position Size in ₹	209292
Qty of shares to be bought	88

Position Size Calc using SL Percent	
Enter your Risk amount in ₹	10000
Enter Buying Price	2365
Enter StopLoss in %	5%
Your Position Size in ₹	200000
Qty of shares to be bought	84

**Risk amount >> Risk amount is the amount you wish to risk for a particular trade, meaning you will lose this amount if trade does not go in your favor & SL hits.

(Fig. 11.2)

So after entering all the values we get the quantity of stocks that can be purchased to 84.

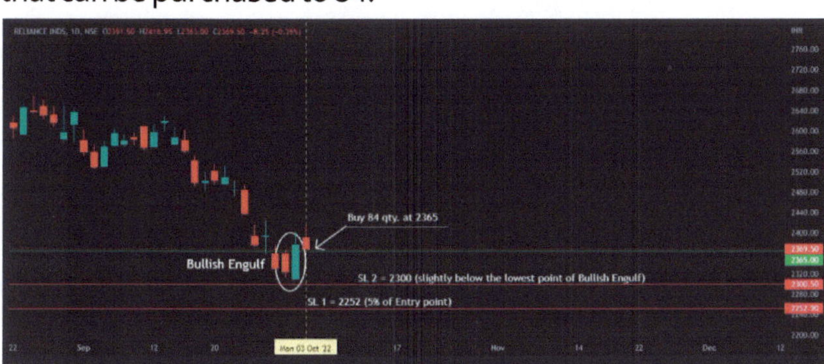

(Chart 72)

So let us summarize the complete entry : Refer chart 72.

Trade setup : Bullish engulf

Stock name : Reliance Industries Ltd. (RIL)

Entry : 2365/- on 3rd October, 2022

SL2 : 2300/- (Risk of 3%)

SL1 : 2252/- (Risk of 5%)

Number of shares bought : 84 nos.

Capital deployed : 2 lakhs

Depending on whether you are a conservative or an aggressive trader, you can use any one of the two stoplosses listed above. You can be in the game for a long time by adhering to the 3% or 5% stoploss rule. Keeping this criterion in mind, if you purchase RIL at Rs. 2,365 and it drops to Rs. 2,252, you would suffer a loss of almost Rs. 10,000 and would need to take the stoploss and exit the position right away. You will only lose 5% of your 2 lakhs capital after taking the stoploss. Take your stoplosses without hesitation. In the stock market, treat them as your lone ally.

Chart 73 shows how the trade that we have taken is working. The market price of RIL as of 01/12/2022, when I am writing this book, is Rs 2,723/-, which is around 15% higher than the purchase level of 2,365/-.

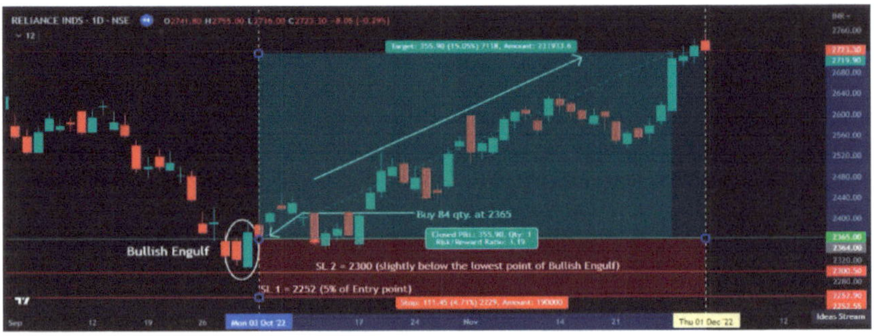

(Chart 73)

So far, in just two months, we have generated profits of almost 15% while only putting 5% of our trading capital at risk.

This has a fantastic risk: reward ratio of about 3.

Once the stock starts to move in your favour, you may trail the stop loss and attempt to capture the maximum move. Once the targeted risk: reward ratio of 1:2 or 1:3 is reached, that would be another point of exit. In this case, closing the trade at the current level of Rs. 2,723/- would be acceptable because the risk: reward ratio of 1:3 was met.

Let me demonstrate the potential of 15% returns, reinvested every two months. Note that pure equity cash delivery market is being discussed here.

Sr. No.	Month	Invested Amount (₹)	Profit at 15% in 2 months (₹)	Risk at 5% Stoploss (₹)
1	Jan	200000		10000
2	Feb		30000	
3	Mar	230000		11500
4	Apr		34500	
5	May	264500		13225
6	Jun		39675	
7	Jul	304175		15209
8	Aug		45626	
9	Sep	349801		17490
10	Oct		52470	
11	Nov	402271		20114
12	Dec		60341	
	Total amount at end of year (Principal + Profits)	**462612**		
	Starting amount	**200000**		
	Returns %	**131.31**		
	Total Profit made in 1 year	**262612**		

(Table 11.3)

Yes!! If you receive modest 15% returns every two months, you might earn a staggering 131% return in just one year. That is how compounding works! This is simply a preliminary estimate to help you see the impact of steady returns of merely 15% over the course of two months.

Pro Tip:

Have a second trading account with Rs. 1 lakh capital and start concentrating on generating a steady return of 15% in 6 trades per year, rather than spending the entire year looking for a single stock to generate multibagger profits. If you strictly adhere to this criteria, I'm confident you'd end up with returns of at least above 50% in a single year.

Please be aware that in the example above, the 131% return is an estimate based on the assumption that every trade was successful. Any stop losses, fees, taxes, or other real-world elements that might affect the actual return are not considered.

The sole purpose of providing this example is to help you understand the value of constantly producing tiny profits rather than occasionally aiming for a large score.

What will happen if the 5% Stop Loss rule is ignored?

The most direct consequence is that you may incur larger losses. Stop loss orders are designed to limit your losses to a certain percentage of your investment. Without this, your losses could potentially be much larger.

Trading without stop loss orders can lead to emotional trading decisions. When a trade starts to go against you, it's easy to hope it will turn around and continue holding onto it. This hope can lead to larger losses if the market continues to move against you. Just imagine how reassuring it would be to initiate a trade knowing the maximum capital you may lose.

Therefore, always keep in mind that position sizing is a crucial and very useful instrument for risk management for any trader.

Another question most people have is that,

What are the criterias for exiting a trade which is already in profit? Or simply put,

When to exit a profitable trade?

The ability to exit a deal profitably allows traders to lock in their gains and control their risk, which is a crucial component of trading. There are a number of factors that traders might consider when choosing when to close out a winning deal. Here are a few of these:

1. **Profit targets:**

   Traders can set a specific price level at which they will exit a trade in order to lock in a certain level of profit. History shows that it is better to book profits once a stocks climbs 20% - 25% after giving a breakout. However, do take into consideration that the stock may continue to climb to greater heights once you exit.

2. **Trail Stop-loss orders:**

   Traders can set a trailing stop-loss order, which is an order to automatically exit a trade if the price falls to a certain level. This helps to limit potential losses in case of an adverse price movement. Also you are able to capture the maximum part of the move. I personally use this in most of my trades.

3. **Risk: Reward ratio:**

   Traders can consider the risk: reward ratio of a trade, which is the ratio of the potential profit to the potential loss. If the potential profit is significantly higher than the potential loss, the trade may be considered worth taking. A risk: reward ratio of 1:2 or 1:3 is considered to be excellent.

4. **Technical indicators:**

   Traders may also use technical indicators such as Moving Average, RSI etc. to determine when to exit a trade. For example, when the stock price crosses a moving average, or when RSI indicates overbought or oversold conditions.

5. **Time-based exits:**

   Some traders may exit a trade after a specific period of time, regardless of the stock's price movement. This is particularly useful for intraday traders.

6. **Market conditions:**

   Traders should also consider the overall market conditions, such as economic events or announcements, and can adjust their exit strategy accordingly.

How to create a Trading Plan-

Creating a trading plan is an important step for any trader to help you make informed decisions and reach your financial goals.

Here are some steps you can take to create a trading plan:

- **Define your goals:**

  Identify your financial goals and the level of risk you are willing to take. This will help you determine the type of trading strategy you should pursue. Goals can be short term or long Term.

- **Identify your market:**

  Research the markets you plan to trade in and identify the assets that align with your goals and risk tolerance. For eg. If you are new, start applying concepts on the Nifty-50 index chart first. Paper trade & see how the market moves are.

- **Develop a strategy:**

  Based on the concepts taught in this book, develop a strategy that outlines how you will enter and exit trades, as well as your risk management methods. Write it down.

- **Test your strategy:**

  Backtest your strategy using historical charts to see how it would have performed in different market conditions. You can also paper trade it before starting with real money.

- **Create a plan for managing risk:**

  Decide on the amount of risk you are willing to take on each trade, and set stop-loss orders to limit your losses. Follow money management rules taught in this book.

- **Monitor and review:**

  Regularly monitor your trades and review your performance. Make adjustments to your strategy as needed based on the market conditions and your own performance.

- **Keep a trading journal:**

  Document all your trades, including entry and exit points, reason for entry and exit, and any emotions or feelings

  that you had while trading. This is what most people refrain from doing. Your trading journal would be helpful in future to only make you a better trader & avoid repeating the same mistakes again.

  It's important to remember that *a trading plan is not a one-time event, but a continual process of monitoring, reviewing, and adapting as needed. The plan should be flexible, so that it can be adjusted as the market conditions and your own goals change.*

Trading Psychology :

Trading psychology refers to the emotional and mental aspects of trading that can impact a trader's decision-making and ultimately affect their trading performance.

Why is Trading Psychology important?

Trading psychology is important in the stock market because it has a significant impact on a trader's behavior and decision-making. Emotions such as fear, greed, and hope can drive traders to make impulsive or irrational decisions, leading to poor performance or even financial losses.

Having a strong understanding of trading psychology can help traders avoid these emotional pitfalls and instead make sound, rational decisions based on market conditions and their own trading plan. A trader who is aware of and can manage their emotions will be less likely to make impulsive trades or hold on to losing positions for too long.

Additionally, having a good understanding of trading psychology can help traders stay focused and disciplined, even in the face of market volatility or losses. This can lead to better performance over the long term, as traders are able to stick to their strategy and avoid making costly mistakes.

In short, *developing a strong trading psychology is an essential part of becoming a successful trader in the stock market.*

Key elements of Trading Psychology :

Some fundamental psychological components that are important for profitable trading are :

1. **Discipline:** The ability to stick to a trading plan and resist the urge to make impulsive trades. Taking stop-loss religiously is a part of discipline.
2. **Patience:** The ability to wait for the right opportunities and not rush into trades. Holding on to a winning trade is just being patient.
3. **Risk management:** The ability to manage risk effectively and protect capital.
4. **Emotional control:** The ability to manage emotions such as fear and greed and not let them cloud your judgment.

5. **Mental fortitude:** The ability to handle stress and maintain a clear head in the face of volatility and uncertainty.
6. **Confidence:** The ability to trust one's own abilities and remain calm under pressure.
7. **Adaptability:** The ability to adjust one's approach as market conditions change.
8. **Continuous learning:** The ability to learn from experiences and continuously improve one's trading skills.

It is important to note that trading psychology is a personal thing, what works for someone else might not work for you. Every individual has to find their own way to manage their emotions and thought process to be successful at trading.

Some Do's & Don'ts in Trading:

1. **Forget the news; Focus on the charts.**

   Remember, there are thousands of other people watching the same news/company results that you are watching. You are not alone.

2. **Do not chase Momentum if you don't know where to exit.**

   Board a running bus only if you know your destination. Just because the bus is full, try to avoid getting in.

3. **Buy the Dips, Sell the Rallies.**

   Buy at key support levels & sell at key resistance levels. In between, you will be butchered.

4. **Trade with the trend. Never go against it,come what may.**

   Never take a position in the opposite direction of an ongoing trend. You will be slaughtered.

5. **After the market opens, wait for the first 15 mins for things to settle down.**

   The first 10-15 mins often reflect the price action of the previous day's traders or BTST (Buy today, Sell Tomorrow).

6. **Bulls live above the 200 EMA levels & Bears live below it.**

   Only Buy the stock if it is above the 200 EMA line in the Daily timeframe. The 200 EMA line is a key dynamic support level for any stock.

7. **Be Greedy when others are Fearful; Be Fearful when others are Greedy.**

   By buying when others are selling and selling when others are buying, you can potentially profit from market movements and minimize your risk.

8. **Beat the crowd in and out.**

   Remember, it's a war between the Bulls & Bears; You have to take money from your opponent before he takes yours.

9. **Don't trust others' opinions.**

   It's your money at stake & not theirs. Do your analysis before entering any trade.

10. **Don't chase hot stocks.**

    Focus only on the charts & forget the press releases. Just because a stock is performing well in the short-term, doesn't mean it will continue to do so.

11. **Do not break your rules.**

    Remember the 2% or 5% SL you have built for your safety. Never break it.

    Consider Stop-Loss as your only friend in the stock market.

12. **Never expect certainty in the stock market.**

    The stock market is uncertain, so never expect certainty in any stock/pattern.

13. **Don't hate losing on any trade.**

    Expect to lose more often than win. Some of the greatest traders in history have an accuracy of 50% or even less than that. Ride your winners & cut off your losers soon enough before they cut you down. That is the only holy grail of trading.

14. **Patience is the key to success.**

    Don't get too caught up in short-term stock price fluctuations. Stay focused on your long-term investment goals. Do remember that the stock market is a tool to transfer money from the impatient to the patient.

15. **First learn, then earn.**

    If you are a new trader, start learning concepts first, then make paper trades & finally, once you are through, only enter the arena. Your initial motive should be survival & not making quick profits. So concentrate on playing the game well, and don't worry about making profits.

BONUS CHAPTER

CHAPTER 12

How to scan for Fundamentally good stocks?

Scanning for fundamentally good stocks involves analyzing the financial and economic indicators of a company to assess its potential for future growth and profitability. Finding innately good stocks requires using stock screeners or stock scanners, searching for financial and economic indicators, assessing the management team of the company, researching the sector, and evaluating financial and economic data.

In this final chapter, we will learn how to scan for *fundamentally good stocks.*

You can create a free scanner using a website called 'www.Screener.in'

Now, creating a scanner requires certain parameters or conditions to be used so that the outcome (innately good stocks) is correct.

So here's a simple, step-by-step guide to building your own scanner at zero cost:

Step 1: Create a free account (or use a Google account to sign in) on 'www.Screener.in'.

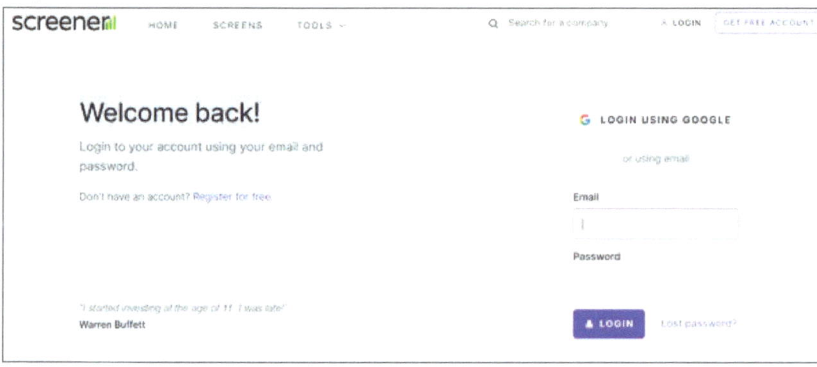

(Step 1)

Step 2: Then go to the Tools section & click 'Create a Stock Screen'.

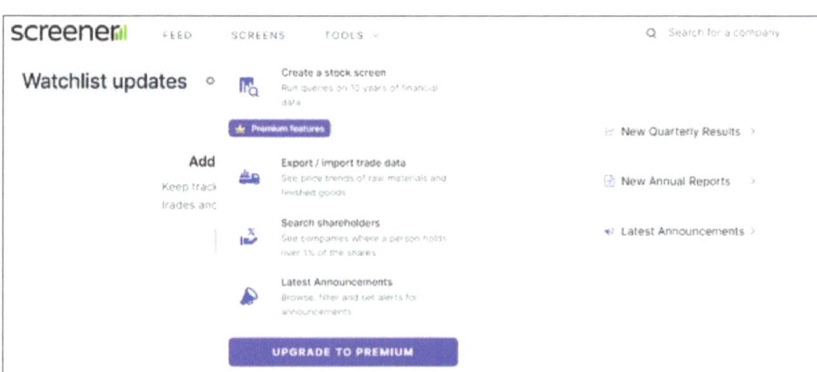

(Step 2)

Step 3 : Now you will see a page where you need to enter the parameters for creating your stock scanner.

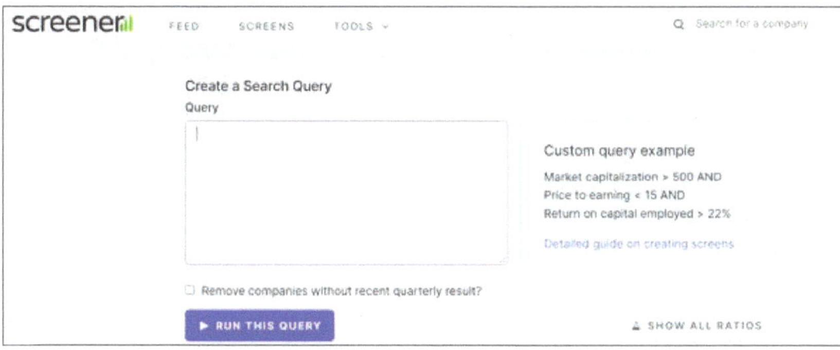

(Step 3)

Step 4 : Next, in the Query Box, you can enter the metrics shown below.

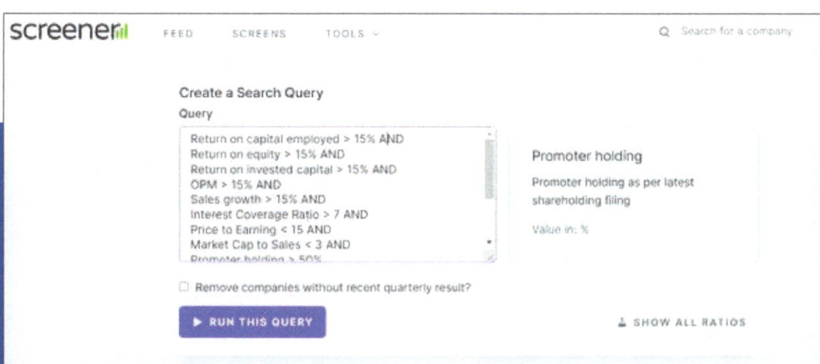

(Step 4)

Note: The parameters for the above metrics can vary for every user. I am sharing the parameters that I use to scan fundamentally good stocks.

- Return on capital employed > 15% (Capital Employed = Share capital + Reserves + Borrowings.)
- Return on equity > 15% (ROE: Return on average equity measures a company's profitability by revealing how much profit a company creates with the money shareholders have invested.)
- Return on invested capital > 15% (Return from Core Business.)
- OPM > 15% (Operating profit margin based on last four quarters.)
- Sales growth > 15% (Sales of previous 4 quarters vs preceding four quarters.)
- Interest Coverage Ratio > 7 (Earnings before Interest and Taxes upon Interest Expense.)
- Price to Earning < 15 (Current Market Price to trailing 12 month's earnings per share.)
- Market Cap to Sales < 3 (Market Cap to Sales ratio.)
- Promoter holding > 50% (Promoter holding as per latest shareholding filing.)

Note: After every criterion, you need to type 'AND' in the query box since you want all requirements validated.

Step 5 : Once this is done, you can Run the query & check out the results. The stocks you will see now would have met all the conditions we had entered.

And now you have filtered 49 fundamentally good stock, out of 1800 stocks listed on NSE , to further apply the Technical analysis concepts that we have learnt in this book.

Query Results

SAVE THIS QUERY

49 results found: Showing page 1 of 1

INDUSTRY EXPORT EDIT COLUMNS

S.No.	Name	CMP Rs.	5Yrs return %	ROCE %	ROE %	ROIC %
1.	EKI Energy	1097.15		236.09	176.17	105.83
2.	Shantidoot Infra	79.00		120.62	161.85	65.60
3.	Kwality Pharma	360.50	44.04	96.81	97.97	57.84
4.	Jainam Ferro	164.40		85.34	64.67	56.39
5.	Castrol India	119.25	-9.66	67.50	49.60	53.91
6.	Balaxi Pharma	567.60	107.24	59.62	53.51	43.88
7.	Sandur Manganese	950.60	17.44	56.78	50.46	46.89
8.	Jindal Poly Inve	429.45	43.90	55.69	54.59	20.34
9.	Godawari Power	379.70	23.25	55.60	52.08	45.86
10.	Maithan Alloys	1023.60	3.09	54.91	41.95	55.60

(Step 5)

- You may design your customized scanner by adding other such parameters as well. Also, there are many pre-designed scanners available on their website.
- Please note that you may get different stocks every time & you can opt for the email facility provided by the website.

Do make a note that I do not intend to promote any particular website related in any way to trading. I have only shared the tools that have helped me in my trading journey. The reader is free to use any website related to trading as per his/her wish.

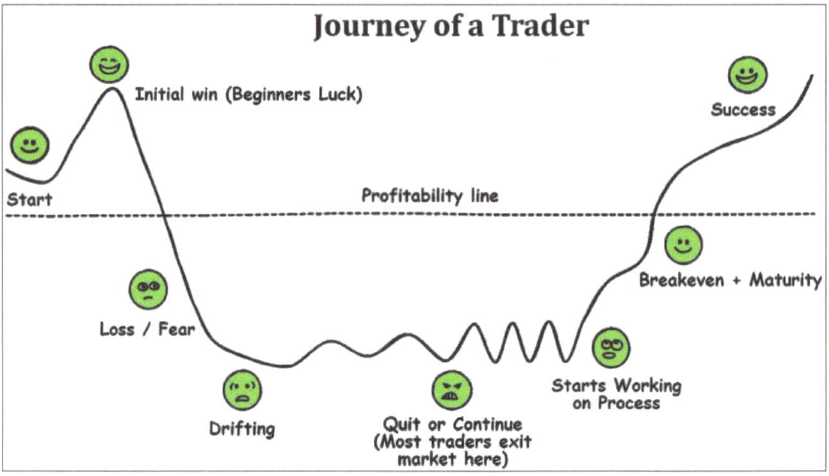

Remember, successful trading is not about finding the 'holy grail' of strategies, but rather about mastering a few tried and true techniques. By learning to read and interpret price action, you'll be well on your way to becoming a consistently profitable trader.

Price action trading is not an easy path, but with dedication and practice, it can be a highly rewarding one. Always remember to manage your risk, stick to your trading plan, and remain disciplined in your approach.

In conclusion, price action trading is not a magic formula for instant wealth. It takes time, patience, and hard work to become proficient in this art. However, the rewards for those who persevere can be significant. So keep studying, keep practicing, and most importantly, never ever stop learning.

Thank you for purchasing and reading my book. I hope you found it valuable and informative. If you have a moment to spare, I would greatly appreciate it, if you could leave a review on Amazon.com or on stocksinvader@gmail.com

Do not forget to follow me on

- @ Akshay Kore https://www.quora.com/profile/Akshay-Kore)
- @stocks_invader -https://www.instagram.com/stocks_invader/)
- @StocksInvader so that we remain connected.
- @www.facebook.com/stocksinvader

WISH YOU ALL THE VERY BEST!!!

Akshay Kore